Praise for **The Floodgates of Anarchy**

"Anyone who wants to know what anarchism is about in the contemporary world would do well to start here. *The Floodgates of Anarchy* forces us to take a hard look at moral and political problems which other more sophisticated doctrines evade."
　　—*The Sunday Times*

"A lucid exposition of revolutionary anarchist theory."
　　—*Peace News*

"Coming from a position of uncompromising class struggle and a tradition that includes many of our exemplary anarchist militants, *The Floodgates of Anarchy* has a power and directness sadly missing from some contemporary anarchist writing. It is exciting to see it back in print, ready for a new generation to read."
　　—Barry Pateman, Associate Editor, The Emma Goldman Papers, University of California, Berkeley

The Floodgates of Anarchy

Stuart Christie & Albert Meltzer

PM Press 2010

The Floodgates of Anarchy by Stuart Christie and Albert Meltzer
© Stuart Christie
This Edition © PM Press 2010

ISBN: 978-1-60486-105-1
LCCN: 2009901386

PM Press
P.O. Box 23912
Oakland, CA 94623
PMPress.org

Printed in the USA on recycled paper.

Cover: John Yates/Stealworks.com
Inside design: Josh MacPhee/Justseeds.org

Contents

Introduction to the 2010 Edition

WE HAVE THREE GOOD REASONS for reissuing this book. First, it was written in the aftermath of the heady events of 1967 and 1968, so that in some sense it completes its third decade of existence this year. If nothing else it is a witness to its time—indeed the dated or obscure references in the text are proof of just that!

Also, Albert is no longer with us in person, and that is sad. A meeting with Albert was a true encounter. He always gave cheer. His obstinacy was never more than caution. His ever-present dedication, common sense, erudition, seriousness, and wit were a delight. Luckily for us, they spring from every page of this book, even those that did not come principally from his typewriter.

Lastly, there still remain hardly any books on the subject of anarchism in relation to the class struggle. Yet with very few exceptions every human being born must fight for survival and dignity from the moment they first draw breath—or someone must do it for them. Even the fortunate few are affected by the plight of the dispossessed masses, living as they do behind the thick skins and the high walls that they need to safeguard their privileges. Since this book was written, those skins may or may not have got thicker, those walls higher. For sure, though, the gap between rich and poor has widened noticeably everywhere. If the ground that has been so lost is ever to be regained, it will only be so when the poor fight back. This book is, we hope, part of that fight.

"What causes war is the meekness of the many," the authors write. Just so. It is the cause, too, of every disaster that befalls the many who are dispossessed. And what causes that meekness is largely the failure of those many to recognise the force within themselves that is the potential to combine to win a better world—by opening "the floodgates of anarchy."

STUART CHRISTIE

Preface

WRITING ON THE SUBJECT of anarchism in relation to the class struggle we had few, if any, books to consult, despite the writings of earlier anarchists when class divisions were taken for granted and before the development of current social and economic trends. The anarchist movement owes little to the writings of the "intellectual"—on the contrary, professional writers have dipped into the achievements of anarchist workers to enlighten themselves on social theory or to formulate other theories.

I was helped in my early thoughts by coming from Glasgow and Blantyre where I grew up amongst miners and others who had kept the socialist and libertarian tradition alive for more than 60 years. I subsequently had the advantage of holding discussions with comrades of the clandestine struggle against Franco such as Octavio Alberola; Salvador Gurucharri and José Pascual Palacios. I must also add to this list Luis Andrés Edo and Alain Pecunia, a fellow prisoner in Carabanchel, Madrid, Prison. Without them and people like them we would have been gobbled up or annihilated entirely by the machinery of the State.

I may say that this book would never have appeared without the help of my co-author Albert Meltzer, a veteran of the anarchist movement for over a third of a century. Albert has worked with stalwarts of a previous generation of British anarchists—Mat Kavanagh, Frank Leech, Albert Grace, Sam Mainwaring Jr., and others—as well as collaborating with revolutionaries in Asia and Europe. Our work in the Anarchist Black Cross, an organization for helping prisoners and activists abroad and in Britain, resulted in this book.

STUART CHRISTIE

★ ★ ★

THE MAJOR BATTLES THAT WE fought in the past were under the red flag of socialism and working-class collectivism. The life's blood of anarchists, too, "dyed its every fold." These colors, together with the battle honors and passwords, have been captured by the enemy. They are now used with intent to deceive.

The classic books about anarchism were written under the red banners. For then socialism had to do with the abolition of exploitation and the establishment of both freedom and equality. The black banners were raised only to call for greater militancy in achieving that goal. In countries such as Russia and Italy, the totalitarian victory was resisted to the bitter end.

The red-and-black banner was first raised in Spain, where the labor movement and anarchism had not parted company, and were almost synonymous. Little has been written on anarchism in relation to the class struggle, and nothing at all (so far as I can discover) in English. The present book is one of the few contemporary writings on what anarchists think, as distinct from academic interpretations as to what they ought to think.

Amongst others I should like to thank Ted Kavanagh for many helpful discussions.

ALBERT MELTZER

Introduction

THE END OF THE First World War saw the growth of super-government. Capitalism, trying to escape the consequences of war, lost its liberal facade. In some cases it had to yield completely to State control, masquerading as communism—which had abolished the old ruling class only to create a new, based not upon profit but upon privilege. In other cases it injected itself with a shot of the same drug, and the nightmare world of fascism was a trip into darkness. The side effect of these experiences was to heighten appreciation of the older form of capitalism. Surely, many argued, the liberal and democratic form of government that capitalism used to provide, and could do so no longer, was a lesser evil? The argument is strangely archaic now, when the growth of the Destruction State means that it is of little significance whether the leadership is bland or brutal; whether it enforces its decisions by unarmed policemen directing protest marchers down empty streets, or turns out the tanks and tear-gas upon them. The issues that are involved today are so vital to the very continuance of mankind that it renders insignificant the fact of whether the maniacs in charge of our destiny come to power via smoke-filled backrooms or by a "whiff of grapeshot."

The State is very clearly our enemy; if we do not destroy it first, it will destroy us. There will be no more national wars on a worldwide scale, or at least, not for long—power-mad clashes will lead to instant destruction. The front-line of the future will confront *us* and *them*. Who are "they" and who are "we"? It may be difficult to define, although we all feel it instinctively. *They* are the dominant class, and those associated with power. *We* are those who are expected to be the pawns of power. They are the dominant class, we are the subjects.

They are the aggressors, but our initiatives to overthrow them are condemned as disturbing the peace. They are the conquerors and we are the conquered, and the failure to define is the result of grass growing over the battlefields. Provided we conform, or try to assimilate, they are content to leave us alone; but even so, they cannot leave the world alone. Those associated with power make their own plans for survival in the event of nuclear war; they may even dream that there are other worlds for them to conquer. To keep us quiet they gloss over the differences within society, and to such an extent that we can hardly tell at times where the division comes. That is the success of the means of persuasion by which, among other instruments of oppression, they exploit us.

One may isolate a section of the ruling class and attack it; but essentially the enemy of man is the means by which he is governed. It is an impersonal instrument although manned by real people. So far back as the ancient Chinese philosophers, it was held that man could not be expected to revere that by which he was chastised and the symbol by which he was made subject (a reasonable expectation later nullified by the Christian church). It was axiomatic to them that the man who sold out to government did so for unworthy reasons. Invited by the emperor to help him rule, one sage asked to be allowed to wash his ears. He was admonished by another sage not to let his oxen drink from the water in which he bathed the ears that had listened to such a proposal.

How can there be antagonism between man and a manmade institution? Because it marks the division of man into rulers and ruled. Is government not merely the administration of society? Yes, but against its will. Society is necessary to unite us; the State, which comes into being to dominate, divides us. Are governments not merely composed of human beings, with all their faults and virtues? Yes, but in order to oppress their fellows. Humanity began with the fact of speech; society began with the art of conversation; the State began with a command.

Government represents the fetters upon society; even at its freest, it merely marks the point beyond which liberty may not go. The State is the preservation of class divisions, and if in that capacity it protects property, it does so in order to defend the interests of a governing class. While this may also entail preserving the lesser property rights of the lower class, at any rate from some inroads, this is merely done to strengthen respect for property. In a society where profit is not the motive, and the class divisions do not determine the economy, the State defends the interests of the bureaucracy.

Even those most concerned with the preservation of a governmental society—the propertied bourgeoisie—are constrained to admit that they do not inevitably get the best of the bargain. The prosperous citizen, with every conceivable need of government on the repressive side, is the more inclined to attack government taking over any other role than that of defending property or curbing working-class activity. Enthralled as he is with the notion of business reciprocity as ethics, he pays his taxes least willingly of all his commitments and sees no dishonor in cheating. Everywhere else, even in his gambling debts, he sees the possibility of something for something, but from the State, nothing.

The State is a parasite upon society. It is ineradicable in a class-divided society, despite the hopes of early liberal capitalists and individualistic philosophers, because the protection of property divisions depends upon organized repression. Once any form of organized repression becomes stronger than any existing form of organized repression, it will take over the functions of the State. Marx (i)[1] analyzed the structure of capitalism clearly enough to perceive that when the necessity for class division was no longer there those repressive institutions *necessary for class rule* would disappear. In the communist countries, however, it can be seen how the retention of *other* repressive organs of the State has meant that far from the State being abolished, it has been strengthened. It has combined the exploitative nature of capitalism with the ordinary repressive nature of the State, and made the latter a greater monstrosity than ever.

The American oil baron, who sneers at any form of State intervention in his manner of conducting business—that is to say, of exploiting man and nature—is also able to "abolish the State" to a certain extent. But he has to build up a repressive machine of his own (an army of sheriffs to guard his interests) and takes over as far as he can, those functions normally exercised by the government, excluding any tendency of the latter that might be an obstacle to his pursuit of wealth. The underworld of Cosa Nostra has, particularly in Sicily and the U.S., built up a State within a State. Granted the necessity for protection from that threat which the Mafia itself presents, it affords as good a bargain as that provided by the State. Were it not there, no necessity for protection would arise. Were the State not there, no necessity for legal curbs would arise, either. There would be no need for constitutional brakes upon power if the people were free.

In the rise of a gangster class, one sees the functions of the State at its crudest. It began "with the crack of the slave driver's whip." It reaches its highest point when it becomes not just the police contractor for the conqueror, but a ruling class in its own right. At that point—and this is sometimes heralded as socialism of the authoritarian type, though it is only done under that banner and could as well be the logical development of capitalism or of fascism—the bureaucrats take over the ministries and the accountants take over the industry. The State becomes not a mere committee for the propertied class, nor even the expression of a dictatorial caste, but a machine perpetuating rule for its own sake and for the aggrandizement of those comprising it. But it is ultimately doomed. The massive concentration of power in a scientific age means the decisions of universal life and death fall into the hands of a few people, accustomed to taking huge responsibilities upon themselves. They cannot imagine that their decisions are not sound ones. They have in their hands the ability to destroy society, and this they will do unless society destroys the State. If the State prevails, the world is doomed. The State being a parasite, it cannot live after it has killed the body on which it feeds.

Like the Great Pyramid, the State was built to the cult of slavery and survives to the cult of death. It has lost all responsibility to mankind; it has lost identity with individual persons and represents a faceless enemy. But it is not *abuse* of State authority that has occasioned this. It is the natural process of maintaining, through the years, division between conquered and conqueror. Civil war is latent in all imposed cultures. The forces of persuasion have blurred the outline of the struggle, but only the conception of the class war makes sense of the economic conflicts in society.

It is no longer fashionable to harp upon class distinctions. Speaking of social change, it is said that the "working class no longer exists." Only when legislation is planned curbing what are alleged to be the malpractices of one class rather than those of another do we find that it is not quite true that "we are all workers now"!

The struggle for class and self-liberation is not to be compared with national conflicts. It is the function of the impersonal State to squander lives in war, or of a superior class to regard lesser humans as expendable; thus any war of the nation-state must in itself be in the nature of an atrocity. This need not be the case in the revolutionary process of breaking down the State, unless intolerable oppression has made people reckless of their own lives and determined to take vengeance (as in Spain in 1936). Those engaged in the struggle for a free society are usually, for that very reason, capable of a heightened appreciation of the condition of others. In any case, their enemies are not whole nations but individuals.

Yet, compared with other conflicts, social liberation is the most difficult of all to achieve, beside which national liberation is a divertissement. For class struggle implies not merely collective action but the breaking down of that sequence of events ingrained in our society as *command-and-obey*. Any form of social protest may be useful as an attempt to destroy this sequence, which saps the lifeblood of mankind and makes it possible for the few to govern the many.

Why, since people must outnumber the minority that comprises the State and its oppressive forces, have they submitted so meekly to it? Why do they quietly queue up to receive their marching orders to war, or to pay their taxes, or to be sentenced to death or forced labor? Society first submitted to the whip—to the armed forces in time of conquest, replaced in a stable society by the police force (or in a less stable society by the army in a police role). Primarily the police force is a method of political repression. Only secondarily is it the means by which, within the legal system, crimes against society are institutionalized by the legalization of some and the outlawry of others. The outlawry of some crimes is, of course, useful if people have lost the initiative to put down antisocial behaviour themselves. This is the aspect of police work used to justify the whole. While it has a degree of inevitability in a State-ruled society, it also has an atrophying effect upon people's initiative to deal with offences against society, and encourages the delinquency it professes to put down.

Since in the long run rule must be by consent, there is in addition to rule by the whip an apparatus of rule by persuasion, by brainwashing and mental conditioning and the whole process of education. It reaches the point where the British people, for instance, might even accept a Gestapo, provided it helped find their lost cats and assisted old ladies across the road.

True education began with an enquiring look; State education began with a salute. The building of a code of ethics and morals suitable for a servile people and adapted to the then current economic system, was originally entrusted to the priesthood, and a church was erected upon the need to subordinate mysticism to power, and to justify the actions of the ruling class. The process of persuasion is much more than the education which conditions the mind to receive it, and runs the whole gambit of national mystique. Education has long since ceased to be the monopoly of the Church, except in isolated corners of the world. In place of the religious organization at the service of the State, and sometimes becoming a parallel State or even master of the secular State, there has been built, in palpable imitation in the totalitarian countries, a hegemonic party in charge of the holy truths (economic or social) that make the system tick. The totalitarian party system comes closer to the old Church, but has no difference with the multiple process nicknamed "the establishment" in countries where there is a diversification of power, and the latter may contain many parties and conflicting interests within the one "Church."

The old Church, and these neo-Churches, may be States within States, super-States, even supra-national States. Their reaction to the State itself, and their inter-reaction to each other, is the essence of what passes off as politics. Their quarrels may become tensions and even wars. These wars may even sometimes follow the lines of the class war, which has driven its furrow through society, but do not produce victories or defeats for the working class, only disasters. Divisions out of time may be preserved, as papal rule petrified the Holy Roman Empire long after its decease. Countries such as Spain still preserve, like dinosaurs in ice, an aristocracy and feudal class fighting against encroaching capitalism.

Similarly, Judeo-Christian morality has been preserved out of time, though suitably modified to conform to the penal code or business habits. (A notable exception is of course the injunction to the children of light to emulate the practice of fraudulent disposition whilst bailee. *Luke* 16. The Bible-worshipping judge of today, who loves money quite as much as any Pharisee, would be equally severe upon this—but it is, sigh the scholars, a difficult passage to translate.) In the main theologians have managed to reconcile Biblical morals with a society that outrages natural justice and propriety, and substitutes property laws. They are thus able to invoke divinity as idealized authority, which is why Bakunin (ii) said that "If God existed, it would be necessary to destroy him."

The nation-state, from being a burden upon society, is elevated by idealistic conceptions—that it derives from God, or alternatively that it derives from necessity—and duties to it are shown as being "in the natural order of things." The cult of nationalism derives from the need to bolster up the sense of duty to the State, just as does established religion. The nation-state is idealized by nationalism, and is shown in a favorable light against other nation-states. This nationalism is an invented ideal supplementing or substituting for religious (or neo-religious, i.e. party or establishment) ideals. It is to mask the unloved and unlovable abstraction of the State with the idealized family of the race or nation.

The feeling of superiority that might be felt for one race over another for historic or purely fictitious reasons, or the inferiority felt (usually for economic reasons) is deliberately confused with one's natural inclination for the people or places one knows best. It is institutionalized into a cult, not merely of nationalism but of a State.

Nationalism is an artificial emotion. It clings around the State like ivy, a parasite upon a parasite. Without a State to twine round, nationalism withers; language becomes dialect, and nationality becomes provincialism, for nationalism is a creature of power. Racialism, not in its usual journalistic sense but the folklore and ethnic traditions of particular peoples, is a plant of hardier growth, and flourishes unless the State takes positive measures to cut it down.

Whereas the creation of a multi-racial or supra-national State leads to an empire (super-State), reaction to it on the purely idealistic ground of race, nation, or difference in religion, is bound to be progressive. It helps to whittle away the bulwark of the State and breaks up the sequence of command-and-obey; but it is only progressive while it is unsuccessful. Hope is said to be a good breakfast but a poor supper. So is the struggle for national independence. The nationalist forms a new State but continues old forms of economic exploitation. By obtaining popular consent to the forms of rule, the new State legitimizes oppression. However, the spirit of rebellion often persists even when nationalism triumphant has taken its dreary course.

All forms of economic exploitation arise from the division between classes and the fact that man is robbed of the full value of his labor. The monetary system is not a mere form of exchange, nor is it properly a science, but a fraud perpetuated by the State in order to legitimize poverty. Capitalist economics is a mystique rather than a science. The science called economics or political economy, wrote Herbert Read (iii), "is the disgrace of a technological civilization. It has failed to produce any coherent science of the production, distribution and consumption of the commodities proliferated by machine production. It has failed to give us an international medium of exchange exempt from the fluctuations and disasters of the gold standard. It is split into a riot of rival sects and irreconcilable dogmas which can only be compared to the scholastic bickerings of the Middle Ages."[2]

Stripped of its bare essentials and uncovered of its ideals—"We have another word for ideals—lies," said Ibsen (iv)—political economy is an apology for civil war, in which one class has economic and political power and the other class is subject. If the latter revolts, it must fight. Since it has submitted and has been mentally processed, collectively and individually, there is some blurring of the division, and an escape clause is granted by which the occasional individual can transcend class barriers and be accepted on the other side. Hence the natural desire for self-betterment is distorted and it is made to appear that one's position in society is the test of one's abilities rather than of one's exploitative value or sheer good luck.

Division is dreaded by the conservative-minded and is equated by them with the fratricidal struggles of the nation-state rather than with the age-old task of trying to get rid of oppressive institutions. For centuries the people have tried nonviolent resistance—or "dumb insolence" as the Army phrased it. (Manipulated enthusiastic participation is a modern invention, though it was implicit in the "bread and circuses" of old Rome.) But nonviolent resistance is not enough. It has no lasting effect even when it becomes armed. A liberal with a gun is still only a liberal. Resistance is a beginning, but it is not enough. All it can do is to break down the sequence of command-and-obey. But resistance only becomes effective when it leads to that breakdown of authority, feared by the authoritarian, which is deliberately confused with the breakdown of all order.

It is with this supposition—that the rule of law prevents disorder—that the revolutionary libertarian quarrels, and this is why he is branded as an *anarchist*. The anarchist believes that the absence of government (anarchy) is freedom. The non-anarchist supposes that the absence of government leads to innumerable disorders normally associated with weak or divided government, where there are the same evils as in strong government, but an absence of unified restraint.

Revolutionary anarchism is not something apart from the working-class struggle. In defining a labor movement, we see no liberty where there is exploitation and no socialism where liberty is lacking. We are for equality without bureaucracy and for a victory of the masses without any ruling faction, old or new.

The generous-minded of the younger generation of the bourgeoisie are apparently more inclined to be with us than against us; they may exercise their right to secede from the rat race and renounce their privileges of birth or connected wealth. We ourselves had nothing to renounce but the illusions of duty with which man has been shackled.

If nowadays we have a little more to lose than mere chains, so much the more reason for making sure of victory. Should the ruling class find it necessary to make a fresh conquest over their subjects (as in Spain), they will take away even that little which we have.

The Class Struggle and Liberty

THE THEORIES OF SOCIAL REVOLUTION have not been produced by theorists, who at most have supplied the technical terms, often at the expense of these becoming looked on as clichés rather than as natural truths. Peter Kropotkin (v) is usually regarded as the main theoretician of anarchism, but he himself wrote upon the subject: ". . . if all of us have contributed to some extent to the work of liberation of exploited mankind, it is because our ideas have been more or less the expression of the ideas that are germinating in the very depths of the masses of the people. The more I live, the more I am convinced that no truthful and useful social science, and no useful and truthful social action, is possible but the science which bases its conclusions, and the action which bases its acts, upon the thoughts and inspirations of the masses. All sociological science and all social actions which do not do that must remain sterile."[3]

The fashionable philosophers of today, whose academic pedantry and class prejudices do not permit them to take note of anybody not mentioned in the university curriculum, will deny that such ideas germinate in the masses and will credit the motivation for social progress to classes of society more congenial to themselves.

It is by no means new to try to reconcile anarchism in terms of Marxism, as is done in the "student debate" of today. Even during the lifetime of Marx, the validity of his economic criticism of capitalism was accepted by the libertarian wing of the International (vi). The International was the first attempt to express the class struggle in terms of an organization based upon the working class. The difference of thinking, as between Marxists and Bakuninists, was a clash between centralism and federalism, and on whether the existing State machinery should be used or destroyed. It is impossible to discuss the capitalist system in terms of changing it without some reference to the work of Marx, and some use of what have now become his clichés, even though the latter have often been used out of context to justify completely different concepts from those intended.

Perhaps to avoid the repeated use of the political cliché we need the skill of the Victorian telegraphist, accustomed to whittle down to two or three words the verbose lucubrations of the bourgeoisie. There is a classical story that, on one occasion during the Crimean War, a general sent a telegram urging that Lieutenant Dowbotham be granted every facility to prove his merits, and that consistent with his military duties it should be borne in mind that his advancement and protection would greatly please those distinguished persons vouching for him. In telegraphese this became "Look after Dowb." So far as modern Britain is concerned, there is no need to think in terms of a conspiracy by the upper classes. Their watchword is still "Look after Dowb." Those who feel that in persisting in using the phrase "class struggle" we are being unutterably banal might reflect on how upper-class endeavors are geared to looking after Dowb. He is guarded if not from the cradle, certainly from the classroom, until the grave (and beyond, as far as the bourgeois historian is concerned).

To look after Dowb from his earliest induction in the public school, he is trained on spartan lines both as a servant of abstract power and a master of lesser humans; he is bred in an elite known to each other in strength and weakness from earliest years, immured to the hardships of power as well as made desirous of it, inculcated in the dominant mystique and way of leadership, and isolated from the rest of the community even at play.

To this day, the "public" school system of education dominates the British ruling class and the task of governing the nation at top level is entrusted to it. Only now has it been possible to envisage a revolt from within, since the continuous absorption of the new ruling class by the old has diluted the latter to a greater extent than was ever thought possible. The capitalist class was welded into the old aristocracy upon the playing-fields of the public schools. Now, a new liberal ruling class is rising from the managerial and technocratic ranks and sensibility and intellect may be found even among the education-fodder. A Shelley (vii) is no longer a total phenomenon in the public school or university. In any case, in modern society he would be treated rather differently. Those who aspire to a gentleman's career in publishing do not go "Shelley baiting," even at school. They wonder how his poetical productions could be used to advantage. Perhaps in advertising?

Even radical Dowb may be looked after nowadays; there are for him the new worlds of the film, radio, TV press, and publicity. There he may enjoy progressive views if he wishes. He can combine his fashionably provocative radicalism with his innate privileges, whilst staid Dowb major pursues the more humdrum road to glory in the Foreign Office or the top echelons of industry.

The sequence of command-and-obey which is preached as high gospel in the education factories is not shattered by more generous views; indeed, the more urbane, who try to bridge the gap between the classes and are specially courteous to those who have not had their advantages may well be the more dangerous.

No longer, of course, is education itself a preserve of the wealthy or those favored by the State. The modern State is too large a monster to be satisfied with trained servants coming from so small a minority. Not only are there wider fields for those trained to rule than ever there were, but the growth of science has created a demand for technicians and scientists. The system of licensed education in turn creates the modern fetish for examinations and the continual polishing and re-polishing of academic learning that goes with them. So we find that some pass their thirtieth birthday, still students, still about to make their contribution to society, doing their academic researches and enjoying their chosen hobbies at the expense of those who work, and the State welcomes it; for the whole purpose of education factories is not to increase the sum of knowledge, but to make docile citizens.

Kropotkin's "typical optimism" was derided when he said that a man need only work until his fortieth year, and then might devote himself to research or science or whatever took his fancy, having performed sufficient value for the community and done his share of the world's work already. [4] But Kropotkin was scientific enough in his analysis and assumptions, and only optimistic in that he believed scientific progress should be used for the betterment of man and not to his disadvantage. He did not believe that this would happen at all if the State were not destroyed root and branch. Because this has not been done, education remains a method of giving a little liberty within the State.

Unfortunately for the bourgeoisie, the process of education cannot be entirely canned and criticism of the present order may creep in. For some take their learning seriously and not all accept their predestined role as trainee mandarins. While the student rebellion may partly be the last outcry of nature before the obsolescence of adult professional life, it is now reasonable to expect that not every student can be bought and sold in the cattle market, and amongst the trainee mandarins there are bound to be some who will reject their destiny in the Destruction State, and it is for these that Cohn-Bendit (viii) amongst others, has become a spokesman.

It would hardly be true to assert, as do some followers of Marcuse (ix) that students form a class of their own. But, in our scientific renaissance, students cannot be charged to do nothing but think about social problems, without coming to some recognition of the basic facts of society and therefore the need for rebellion. The young automatically question established authority. Some enthusiastic Tories think that the answer to student militancy is to cut off their grants. But even the ultra-Toryism of an Abdul the Damned—to cut off their heads—would not suffice. The system will not stand up to scrutiny. The "queen of the sciences" in specific universities may still be the classical queen, theology; it may be the drag queen, economics; or the lady-president of the sciences, Marxist-Leninism in Eastern Europe—or the American equivalent, social and business administration. But now they must buy out or abdicate. The ruling class must woo and win the trainee mandarins; the current asking prices are advertised in the columns of the better Sundays. They are well in advance of thirty pieces of silver, and may even be accepted without the need for selling out. You object to using your degree for destructive nuclear research? Why not try the social services?

At present, Marx's analysis that the ruling class is sustained by the surplus value produced by the working class, very largely holds good. We still live in a competitive society, though its edges are becoming blurred by collectivism. Labor is bought and sold like anything else. The myth of capitalism is, of course, that one gets what one deserves; those who do well out of the system like to believe that it is their superior intellect that is the cause. The Conservative credo is that without some reward, society would go flat. The same people protest indignantly when they find that "after their expensive education and training" perhaps "a dustman" is doing as well as themselves. They do not like the logical application of the competitive system which is that everything is bought and sold, and in the cheapest market possible. If there is a superfluity of doctors, down will go their wages in proportion to the national level. If nobody wants to become a dustman, the dustman's wages will rise, unless forcibly kept down by the State. This has been a reason for government intervention in industrial matters since the Black Death caused laborers' wages to rise, and legislation artificially lowered them.

Abolition of competition is not enough. In a non-competitive society, such as we have had in the past and are likely to have again (the Jesuit state of Paraguay or the communist countries today) the relationship of classes will still be to the benefit of those with power. Property relations have, after all, changed in the "communist" countries and classes are theoretically no more. Still, no fair observer could deny the continuation of the class system, and even those who pretend "the class struggle no longer exists" in the Soviet countries must see that while the big capitalists and landlords have vanished, and only small owners, especially small farm owners, remain (and even these face disappearance as the State extends its monopoly) yet there are quite obviously classes of some sort. Though in Russia the "capitalist" in the Marxian sense is an anachronism, and exists only on the very periphery of the economy, market trading (with illegal overtones), there is no social equality. Classes certainly exist in the sense used by sociologists to denote distinct social strata based upon different levels of income and occupation, and also in the sense of the dispossessed against the rulers, even if they no longer exist in the older sense.

In so far as this division of classes is concerned, not only is there no socialism in Russia, but the signs of it being wanted anywhere in the counties are less than ever. The working class, deceived for so long as to what socialism is and on the nature of the class struggle, uses such phrases in the way that the Christian mouths phrases without grasping their content. The Soviet underprivileged look for economic betterment individually or collectively, and lavish praise on those individual rulers who will give a little more liberty in some matters. In some of the satellites it is only necessary to do a little flag waving for the ruling class to be regarded with favor.

The Communist Party in these countries merely sets the tone for a careers pyramid, based upon a different set of values from those of capitalism, and yet fundamentally coming back to the lie of rewards for service; the sham need for obedience and duty; and the superimposition of self-sacrifice when the needs of the State demand it.

It is in this respect that Russian Marxism has parted company with the Maoists, the Chinese brand of Marxist-Leninism. This wing clearly recognizes the existence of class struggle both in capitalist and "communist" countries. They tend, in the capitalist countries, to be more progressive than the orthodox communists, who deny class struggle and think only of the national needs of Moscow. Although the Maoists claim to be in the tradition of Stalin, they are in fact more revolutionary than those communists who have thrown over the Stalinist myth, and as regards the Soviet Union, the Maoists proclaim revolutionary opposition much more clearly than the timorous Trotskyists were ever able or willing to do. Whereas Trotsky (x) blamed Stalin personally, or "the bureaucracy," but insisted that Russia was "the workers' state," the Maoists understand there is a class struggle in Russia and its satellites, and even in China.

However, since they are themselves in power in China, it would be too much to expect them to realize that in *that* country the enemy of man is the means by which he is governed. They perceive the divisions in their regime, but conclude that it is due to their own shortcomings as a bureaucracy, and preach self-criticism to the point where it becomes absurd. They strive to eliminate "bourgeois relics" in their own party, thinking that by a "cultural revolution" they will be able to reconstruct the party and shake off the bad habits it no doubt acquired during the struggle against capitalism. They fail to see that what oppresses the masses is not so much the *habits* the party acquired under capitalism, bad as they may be, but the *powers* they have acquired since. They cannot introduce an anti-authoritarian regime except by abolishing themselves, and though this may be the theory of Marxism, it will never be the practice, for power readily convinces its possessors of their own indispensability.

They are revolutionary in every country but their own, like the Victorian bourgeoisie. They represent socialism without liberty—which in Bakunin's formula, means tyranny, just as liberty without socialism means exploitation.

With this "liberty" without socialism we in the West are familiar. It is seen in the plea of the private-enterprise capitalist to be left alone by the State to make money and keep it. But he does not entirely reject the State; he merely despises it, as the public hangman was once despised and rejected by the supporters of capital punishment. If anything is run by the government it cannot be any good, he says, but he calls for greater punishment by government of those who interfere with his profit-making and safety. At the height of his individualism, in the middle of his boasts as to the manner in which he left his former employment to start on his own "to better himself" and never looked back (or beneath) he wants the government to take legal sanctions against those who leave his own factory gates to go on strike to better their own lot.

This "liberty," too, is the "national" form which consists in the right to have the same tongue as the otherwise faceless rulers. It is the "liberty" one defends when one has surrendered every civil liberty to become a soldier. It is the classical "liberty" to starve on a park bench or to dine at the Ritz, modified today by the fact that the State will readily take charge of the vagrant and so enable the expense-account diner to sup at the Ritz with a comfortable conscience.

It is the "liberty" to say whatever one chooses, within reason (that is to say, within law) provided one does nothing effective about it. Cant about liberty may always be recognized; it is accompanied by a hope that liberty will not become "license," that is to say, that it will never be real freedom, and that nobody will take advantage of benefits really intended for those conferring them. It is "liberty" for politicians to criticize each other, and a breach of privilege for us to criticize them when they do not feel like it. It is "liberty" for judges and magistrates to express their prejudices; it is "contempt" for us to reveal our contempt.

Law is not liberty. The most progressive laws merely mark the boundaries beyond which liberty may not go. To express social change in terms of law means a defeat in the class struggle, not a victory; it facilitates the rise of a new ruling class, or renders the old one more capable of withstanding supersession.

All classes may be revolutionary. All are capable of making great changes and reforms. All may, in their time, be progressive, and degenerate only with changing conditions. But only productive classes can be libertarian, because they do not need to exploit others, and do not need, therefore, to maintain either the machinery of exploitation, or the means by which others can be forced or persuaded to give up their liberty in return for real or imagined protection.

The Road to Utopia

WE CAN HARDLY DECLARE ourselves unconditionally for unbridled freedom and then go on to lay down blueprints for the future. We are not clairvoyants to be able to predict the social and economic structure of a free society. It is not possible to lay down rules as to how affairs should be managed when the management of mankind itself is abolished. But at the same time, the rebel in this society cannot be patient enough to wait for an expression of spontaneity as if for the Messiah. He has to choose a programme of action and the road to utopia. There may be more than one way, and we may need to shift our course, but the knowledge of where we want to get enables us to pursue a consistent course at the moment.

If our aim is the abolition of the State, it does not make good sense to think of forming a new state when the capitalist state is abolished, still less to establish a dictatorship. This, of course, was a fallacy of Lenin's (xi), whose programme of action was geared up to the circumstances of the First World War (and not to utopia), and whose theoretical conclusions were bound up with the conquest of power by his party. He sought to justify this in socialistic terms. The "soviets," workers' and soldiers' councils, and the local communities of peasants, were already in control when the Bolsheviks (xii) returned to Russia. He retained the name, but in practice applied it so loosely that today the term "soviet" is little more than a synonym for the Russian Empire.

Lenin advocated the "withering-away of the state," in Marxist traditional language, though to an extent which surprised contemporary Marxists in the social-democratic movement (who felt he was "trying to steal Bakunin's thunder"). He pursued an entirely different road to one which would lead to the end of government.

He strengthened the repressive force of government and abolished only those organs of the state which existed exclusively to enforce the competitive system. By doing this he was ultimately working to the same goal that other Marxist social-democrats had in mind, and may have been wiser in his generation than they. German Marxism would have led to the same reality as Russian Bolshevism, perhaps in a less brutal fashion, perhaps not. Both diverged from the class struggle. They aimed at re-imposing the rule of one superior section of the community upon another, and replacing party rule for the old rule. The party in Russia became a bureaucracy and the bureaucracy became a new ruling-class. In the sense that it works for wages and not for profit, it is not a capitalist class, but it is a higher social class and could hardly be called a productive one.

Many of those who opt out of the class struggle, or frankly change sides, do so because they see only too clearly the grimness of state communism, in which the State is all and the community nothing. But the fact that it suits Russian and Chinese imperialism to claim that the interests of their respective governments are parallel with those of the international class struggle, does not make them so, any more than the claims of the American and British governments to represent democracy need be regarded seriously. Without the idea of what the struggle is about, without the vision of utopia, the struggle is lost.

Few can do without the vision of utopia. It is true the vision varies. It was a German militarist who felt that universal peace was "a dream, and not even a good dream," and the militaristic utopia was for him typified by Valhalla. The authoritarian pictures his ideal society as one in which he has only to breathe a command, and the world jumps to its feet to obey. Unfortunately, this is not entirely a dream. It is true that, so far as their personal ambitions are concerned, most authoritarians recognize it as a fantasy. But though they may never hope to achieve complete authority themselves, they work towards an authoritarian ideal. In this pursuit they may support tougher prison sentences or the reform of prisons (the second is only the more tolerant version of the first). They may advocate corporal punishment or the death penalty, or according to their political opinions, support nationalization of industry or strong central government. All are aspects of authoritarianism falling short of the complete state-fantasy. Naturally, according to more or less liberal opinions, the authoritarian may differ on these concepts, so that those who want *one* conclusion do not necessarily want the *other*.

Some professional people, who predominate as Labor MPs, see their utopia as the welfare state; a glorified housing committee run by experts and modified by advice bureau, with themselves as wise and kindly fathers of the people. Meanwhile they settle for reforms in this direction, some of which may be good, but they all lead to Big Brother. Oh the other hand—very much on the other hand—there are those who see the nation reformed in the manner of Craft's Dog Show, as a racial utopia; meanwhile they settle for nagging immigrants about their degree of sun-tan. Other authoritarians may have the vision of that Czar who drilled his soldiers to perfection and then had but one complaint: they still breathed.

Those who reject authoritarianism will require nobody's permission to breathe. The libertarian owes no duties or allegiance; is not grateful for permission to reside anywhere on his own planet and denies the right of any one to screen off bits of it for their own use or rule.

The libertarian rejection of all authority may amuse or terrify the shepherd, according to the degree of self-confidence or the militancy with which it is put forward: it invariably provokes consternation among the sheep. What would life be like without the shepherd? They bleat, their dismay heightened even more by the fact that they hate and detest the shepherd, whom they know ultimately intends to slaughter them. But the startling supposition that they could exist without him implies that generations of mutton-yielding were in vain.

Objections to a free society, one without repressive institutions, come even from those who pay lip-service to the idea that the state itself is an evil, even if thought of as a necessary one. They have similar underlying assumptions, the most frequent of which is that there is no alternative to coercion of one sort or another, and that all social problems must be solved by compulsion—either legal sanctions or economic pressures. "Who will do the dirty work?" they demand of the anarchist, implying that either some must be starved in order to do what they regard as uncongenial; or else that the government must force people to do it (on the lines of wartime direction into the mines or military conscription). Although this argument is intended to demonstrate the alleged impossibility of freedom, it is equally a criticism of any form of general prosperity. It is why outspoken Tories (those with safe electoral seats in areas where support for unemployment as a policy will not be unpopular) demand a margin of worklessness. Society finds it difficult to answer the question as to who will do uncongenial jobs if there is neither industrial conscription nor the spur of starvation. At present, the democratic state postpones the problem by a shuffling around of populations causing the less popular work to be done by the more recently arrived people.

Another assumption is that there is no logical alternative to government but lunacy, and this is even held when, as has not infrequently been the case, the government is in the hands of raging lunatics anyway. It is believed that society would, in the absence of government, allow any maniac to dominate and kill, or persuade people to do so to each other, and all that prevents this is the restraining hand of an institutionalized legal system. But to see that this is a fallacy, one need only read the crime news. It is the legal system itself which allows maniacs to dominate and kill, collectively or individually, as part of command-and-obey, and which allows them to get into positions where they can either act in defiance of other people's law or alternatively where they can fashion the law for themselves.

When an anarchist position is placed before those who have never previously questioned authority as such, they show the fear of the modern jungle which normally they sublimate. Like the fictional pygmy people of the forest, they look to Tarzan to protect them from the terrors of the jungle, however much they may normally criticize their governmental Tarzan. Take away Boss-Tarzan and they see themselves isolated in the jungle. They do not comprehend that there can be a jungle pruned, cultivated, civilized; a situation in which Tarzan is unnecessary for their protection, and in which it becomes clear he is only there to exploit their labor.

"Thieves and maniacs would beset us!" cry the supporters of government. "Our wives would be raped, our property taken, we would be murdered!" But all that happens to them in the jungle, despite Tarzan, often through his connivance, and sometimes directly by him. It does not happen in the cultivated garden of which they have no experience. In the jungle in which we live, murder is recognized as such only by virtue of whether it has been legalized or not, and the primary motive of the ambitious is self-aggrandizement at the cost of others. When the ambitious have power, they preach self-sacrifice by others. (Be "restrained," be patriotic, have the "national" interest at heart). Of those who sacrifice, it can only be said they lose out in this system. For the only means of independence in the jungle is by the possession of property, by cornering a portion of the community and using it for personal ransom. Proudhon (xiii) was not in the least guilty of a contradiction, as some pedants think, when he said that *property was theft* but that it was also liberty. It is like a gun, useful in the jungle and the only means of preserving independence within it, but nevertheless anti-social the moment a society escapes from the jungle.

The free society cannot know anything of special property rights any more than it can of privilege, hereditary or acquired, for special liberties for *some* imply less for *others*, and competition for betterment at the expense of others can only be settled by force. The necessity for the system of ownership of property at present is in order to corner the market in necessities and to hold the community to ransom. The community, being the greater, will not be held to ransom unless some repressive machinery (force or persuasion) makes it do so.

By cooperative production the natural wealth of the world can be available to all. This would only be a mixed blessing if government still existed. The inevitable tendency of government is to create special privileges for itself and so re-establish inequities. Where would the delights of public life be without the serfs marching past to salute; or the flag-bedecked limousines, or the dignified jaunts at the public expense? The government, being itself by nature a privileged class, must introduce—if these ever went—the system of rewards and incentives that persuade others of the necessity and the joys of obedience. This is exactly what has happened in Russia, but is paralleled in the Western countries, too. The measure of independence is that one does not need others to grant one rewards or allow one incentives. These are given to inferiors. What small shopkeeper today, for instance—without some ingenious tax fiddle, at least—would gravely allow himself an overtime bonus of a pound a week, to be deducted from his own profit? It would be equally absurd for the worker if he controlled his own factory.

Free cooperation naturally leads to decentralization, and possibly the ending of a lot of large-scale production which is the joy and pride of monopoly, whether capitalistic state or even cooperative. The craftsman nourishes in a free society, when the building of pyramids or vast office blocks falls into disuse.

Workers' control is a question of economic freedom. It has nothing in itself to do with morality or ethics, which are quite different problems. The old conservative criticism, that men must be angels before they will work together like men, is echoed in the plea of the Christian Socialist for moral perfection before utopia is possible. Here is Charles Kingsley's address to the Chartists:

You have more friends than you think for. . . . You may disbelieve them, insult them—you cannot stop them working for you, beseeching you as you love yourselves, to turn back from the precipice of riot, which ends in the gulf of universal distrust, agitation, stagnation, starvation. . . . but will the Charter make you free? Will it free you from slavery to ten-pound bribes? Slavery to beer and gin? Slavery to every spouter . . . ? That I guess is real slavery, to be a slave to one's own stomach, one's own pocket, one's own temper. Will the Charter cure that? Friends, you want more than Acts of Parliament can give . . . there can be no true freedom without virtue . . . be wise and you *must* be free, for you will be *fit* to be free.[5]

There is no doubt much good sense in all this, but it is insufferably patronizing and is untrue as far as the particular aims of the Chartists were concerned. For the middle classes were free enough within the limits of what the Charter demanded, though they were slaves enough to their stomachs, pockets, tempers, and spouters. Far more so, one might have thought, than the Victorian working classes. From Kingsley's approach, rejected by the materialist socialist, sprang the common modern fallacy that revolutionary socialism is an "idealisation" of the workers and that the mere recital of their present faults is a refutation of the class-struggle which (it is again supposed) can only exist if a Kingsleyan idealized proletariat can be proved to exist. Poor Kingsley! His dictum that "religion is the opium of the people," quoted by Marx and usually attributed to Lenin, has also been generally misunderstood. Opium was then used in operations when the pain was too unbearable, since anesthetics were unknown, and evangelical religion was also resorted to when existence became otherwise unbearable.

This attitude has passed over as an inheritance to the peace-movement liberal, who finds himself in the libertarian camp for purely political reasons (disillusion with politics or a recognition that "war is the health of the state"). To the Christian Socialist or his secular equivalent it seems morally unreasonable that a free society, still thought of in terms of "reward" or "privilege" could exist without moral or ethical perfection. But so far as the overthrow of society is concerned, we may ignore the fact of people's shortcomings and prejudices, so long as they do not become institutionalized. One may view without concern the fact that bothers the advanced liberal; that the workers might achieve control of their places of work long before they had acquired the social graces of the "intellectual" or shed all the prejudices of the present society from family discipline to xenophobia. What does it matter, so long as they can run industry without masters? Prejudices wither in freedom and only flourish while the social climate is favorable to them. The Israeli kibbutzim are an example of people working in free conditions, despite advanced patriotic or religious prejudices which make them far from libertarian in their relationships to people outside. What we say is, however, that once life can continue without imposed authority from above, and imposed authority cannot survive the withdrawal of labor from its service, the prejudices of authoritarianism will disappear. There is no cure for them other than the free process of education, and the disappearance of rule-by-persuasion.

Free education has already progressed in this direction. The pioneering work of A.S. Neill (xiv), nurtured in private schools for a very small minority, went on to influence a whole generation of teachers. But however much progressive views on education are important from the point of view of a child's happiness, and even today help to alleviate the bigotries and hatreds of school life, they can only ultimately enable the pupil to integrate into present-day society.

Today, an increasing number of teachers and pupils recognize that this is not enough. Allied to free education must be the movement to alter society. It is not enough to abolish examinations, one has to alter a competitive society. It is not enough to abolish classroom dictatorship, it is necessary to abolish governmental discipline. From the Neill movement has grown the movement of pupils, from classroom alliances to student associations, which understands that education has always been subservient to the ruling economy, and which is not content only to make the paths of education more pleasant but also wants to make its education applicable to life in a free society.

Least of all does it concern itself with the facts of discipline or otherwise, with which the do-gooders feel it should be solely concerned. It is not solely a question of standing up against intolerant teachers, or tolerant ones with jobs to consider, but tolerance and intolerance are only different sides of the coin of authoritarianism. Nobody in his senses says that he has an objection, or that he does not have any objection, to Scotsmen coming to Great Britain. It would be idiotic, for the question of tolerance and intolerance does not arise; they are there as a right.

To the libertarian, the world in his own. Those who have superior force may, according to nature, be kindly and generous or despotic and illiberal, but they are our enemies. Though naturally most people prefer to have a more generous enemy in the saddle, they survive the longest. The growth of fascism made the situation more complicated. The despotic and illiberal became so dominant, and the generous so rare, that the latter seemed like a port in the storm. But with all their tolerance, the liberals will, in a crisis, betray their posts, for in times of stress they see "the floodgates of anarchy" opening. History has shown how the liberal will call in the army when things get tough, knowing that it will cause the downfall of democracy, but preferring that to revolution. General Franco was a paid Army officer on the salary list of the Republican Government he destroyed. The "impractical" anarchist movement, the CNT-FAI (xv) called for the abolition of the Army and fought against it. The socialists and republicans preferred to bring in "reliable" Army officers, such as General Franco, with his Masonic background, replacing the monarchist officers. The Republic felt that this would save them from both fascism and the workers. The result is well known.

In a like manner, faced with the possibility of a postwar revolution all over Eastern Europe, once the Nazis had been defeated, Mr. Churchill and Mr. Roosevelt preferred to sell the lot out to Soviet Russia, "the devil they knew" to which they had always been implacably opposed, rather than the devil of social revolution they did not know but feared all the more. Anything was better than the "floodgates of anarchy" so far as they were concerned. So far as we are concerned, these are the gates which have to be opened.

The Labor Movement

ANARCHISM AS A MOVEMENT in its own right has its own traditions, now a century old, yet forms a faction within the international labor movement as a whole. It has its particular inheritance, part of which it shares with socialism, giving it a family resemblance to certain of its enemies. Another part of its inheritance it shares with liberalism, making it, at birth, kissing-cousins with American-type radical individualism, a large part of which has married out of the family into the Right Wing and is no longer on speaking terms.

To understand anarchism, it is necessary to understand the parting of the ways in the labor movement, by which term is not implied the Labor-TUC cooperative set-up; though this is also part of it, and happens in Great Britain to be the dominant tendency.

The anarchist tradition has its own martyrology, sometimes shared. There are the Chicago Martyrs (xvi); Sacco and Vanzetti (xvii); Joe Hill of the IWW (xviii); and a roll-call of heroes as well as a record of successes and failures. But if it is unsatisfactory, except by way of inspiration, to judge a movement by the spontaneous devotion it inspires (which can be said of many evangelical sects, though noticeably lacking in the established parties and religions of today), it is equally so to consider a movement, not based on rigid party lines, merely on the basis of the success and failures of those who happen to be its current adherents. To gauge "the anarchists" in terms of somebody who happened to do something or other at any particular date, is to affirm the obvious, that in the absence of rigid party lines to conceive a movement too broadly means one will include not only its heroes but those who may not necessarily measure up to its tenets. This is inevitable if one rejects, even assuming it were feasible, the ideal of legal copyright in a name.

Fortunately, a certain shock-therapeutic value in the connotation of "anarchist" with "terrorist" has preserved it, by and large, from becoming as debased as the once great names of "radical," "socialist," "liberal," "communist." Only when a faint tinge of radicalism is acceptable does the liberal, advanced in ideas but indisposed to action, care to make use of the name, and then usually qualified with a hyphenated dilutive (anarchist-pacifist, philosophic-anarchist, anarchist-individualist) that does not jar too much in the literary, artistic or academic world. The diluted-anarchist is more absent among the scientific intelligentsia where profession of belief would require a stand to be made. An artist, on the other hand, might be forgiven the use of the name—it might even be expected of him. He can hang his pictures in the Royal Academy and even paint the Queen (as did the late Augustus John) without disguising his opinions. It would be a bold scientist who stated his dissent while working among the establishment.

It has been cynically observed that, despite the wealth of the anarchist tradition, every young generation that finds the way to anarchism for itself, and not by way of introduction from others, falls into the delusion of being the first to discover it. By extension the hippies believe they were the first ever to drop out of society. This Columbian delusion is harmless enough, except historically; to it the generation of the sixties, or at least its outside interpreters, has faithfully adhered. Dutschke (xix) has re-stated, and the discovery re-echoed around the militant world, the case for council communism, often distorted today by Maoist or Ho Chi Minhite phrases which express a confusion of thought in opposition phraseology. It is also sometimes referred to as "anarcho-Marxism," as if this were a modern amalgam resolving ancient antagonisms. Again this is misleading, as anarcho-syndicalists (anarchists within the labor movement) always accepted Marx's economic criticisms and analysis and disagreed with Marxism only on the need for legalism, political leadership, the question of State control or the role of the party. All this is exactly what is accepted by "anarcho-Marxists," like Cohn-Bendit, from the anarchist tradition.

It is true, however, to say that the Marxist tradition in the working class, at the point which it reached among the Spartacists (xx), for instance, becomes indistinguishable, except in phrases or associations, from anarcho-syndicalism. It may, when deriving from a more genuine proletarian tradition in particular countries, be more revolutionary than an anarchism still identified, at too late a period, with the trade union type of organization, or divorced from the struggle as an ideo-logical union and nothing more.

The tradition of working-class association stems from the guilds of craftsmen in the Middle Ages and was developed in the struggle against industrial capitalism. Trade unionism was obviously the first step forward in the Industrial Revolution, as a means of defense, and of representing the organized workers against their immediate oppressors. The fact that, in the type of trade unionism of which the TUC is now a model, there was an institutionalized or parliamentarian leadership, did not prevent economic advances being made. Many of the trade union pioneers, including some who later became reactionary, were socially progressive for a period. Local militancy was always able to keep trade unionism an effective force whatever the leadership, but the First World War brought the first major showdown. Until then it was of less importance that the leadership was reformist than that union solidarity should grow, unless the leadership positively inhibited the growth of the union. This, for instance, happened in the American labor movement, which, by its insistence on craft unionism, originally adapted to the facts of the seventies and eighties, became by the turn of the century so divisive as to be powerless.

The British trade union leadership, influenced by the Fabians (xxi), generally depended upon legislation rather than direct action to bolster up their effectiveness. They turned first to the radical wing of the Liberal Party, and then to their own candidates, who later linked with the social-democratic movement to form their own Labor Party. The American trade unions, on the other hand, lacking both Fabian and revolutionary influence, left the social-democratic movement to its fate as a sectarian party that waxed and waned to a shade. They had a distaste for politics as recognizably corrupt and turned to bargaining with the employers on a purely commercial basis. This naturally brought into being, as well as the giant company-type unionism of to-day, also the gangster-controlled union (crime is after all a business like any other) which competes for favor in the goods it can deliver, with the "clean" union that sells its rulebook for cash gains and whose bosses set their salaries according to their "opposite numbers" in industry.

With the boom expansion of American capitalism, in a period of uninhibited technological advance, and with the rest of the world reduced by war, the American worker has thus become the highest paid and least powerful in the world. Remembering his helplessness in time of depression, he is all the more inclined to conform during the period when his helplessness is at least paying off in high wages and good living. Those who artificially produced the slump have now artificially produced prosperity. His attitude is that of Napoleon's mother to the First Empire: "It's all right, as long as it lasts."

In France the trade union movement grew up in quite a different atmosphere. At the turn of the century anarchism was at least as popular as state socialism among the French workers. The antipolitical theory competing with the parliamentarian for influence, it was natural that in a period of struggle the former should come more to the fore, though acknowledgements must be made to the work of Pelloutier (xxii) in the CGT. The labor movement wished to achieve independence from the State, and set as its task not merely the economic betterment of the workers by direct action, but also the control of each industry by those working in that industry. The French word for trade unionism, *syndicalisme*, became synonymous internationally with that form of labor organization which abjured parliamentarism and set up workers' control as the road to utopia.

The French workers had perfected the strike weapon and all forms of industrial struggle, including the occupation of the factories—to which, years later, in 1936 and again in 1968, they returned, long after parliamentarism had appeared to prevail. It was their view that the social general strike would be no more than an occupation of the factories, after which the workers would resume work but keep the employers and the State locked out. This becomes more than occupation. It is expropriation—the final challenge to capitalism.

In Italy, such an occupation of the factories in the 1920s was answered by the bourgeoisie, although disposed to liberalism, turning in despair to fascism to rescue the capitalist system from expropriation. The current phrase is "right-wing backlash." In Spain, where social-democracy was a latecomer, the labor movement was mostly anarchist, and the workers responded to what was intended as an army takeover to prevent social expropriation, by the greatest force at their disposal, the social revolution itself. The ruling class retorted with the greatest force at its disposal, genocide. The original Dollfuss-type fascism became civil war by the ruling class against its own people, which is the class struggle in its crudest form.

In the United States there was a reaction to narrow craft unionism when the Industrial Workers of the World (xxiii) was created. It was influenced by French syndicalism, possibly at second hand, by Italian immigration, by native American radicalism, by East European anarchism and to a small though perceptible extent, by the theories of Daniel De Leon (xxiv). It was part of the syndicalist development throughout the world that influenced American, Australian and some British thought on the need for worker's control within the socialist society. It showed how the new society should be "created within the shell of the old" by industrial unionism. This prototype of revolutionary labor thinking was in direct contrast to the parliamentarian labor idea current in the British trade unions which had created the Labor Party. Fabian influence, which had pushed them in the direction of the Liberal Party, re-created the image of the latter in the new party.

The role of the trade union leadership in bargaining directly with capitalism and using working-class militancy, or at least the threat of it, as a lever, has nowadays been challenged by social-democratic politicians who want to make the unions into bargaining agencies of the State. This trend first emerged in the First World War, when the alleged national exigencies gave the government the chance to curb the labor movement. Only the militancy reintroduced by the short-lived British syndicalist movement and the IWW saved the working class from a complete collapse into industrial serfdom, from which the declaration of peace would not necessarily have saved them.

In that war, those who had always applauded the value of a free market and the ability of unfettered enterprise to deliver the goods, and indeed still let the manufacturer go on making profits in order not to interfere with the sacred rights of property, were quite adamant that the working class had to sacrifice if the nation were to be triumphant. The parliamentarian leadership of the unions immediately capitulated. In Britain it collaborated, in Germany it obeyed. In both countries it began the long, disastrous course of accepting State intervention in industrial affairs.

In Britain this was the logical consequence of Fabian influence. In Germany the socialists had denied there were any great possibilities in the union movement anyway. Lassalle (xxv) had formulated his Iron Law of Wages, popular again nowadays among the economists, by which it alleged that if wages went up, so did prices, and all union activity was a vicious circle.

As a result, the trade union movement in both countries was held to be useless to its membership, so far as any prospect of defending their living standards was concerned. All strikes became "unofficial"—a curious phrase, suggestive of an alternative possibility of licensed rebellion. When the workers turned to the trade union movement, for defense of their living standards, they found it was incorporated in the State. But in every factory the shop steward, who had up till then been a collector of dues from the worker on behalf of the trade union and no more (though this in itself, during an anti-union period, had been a job requiring guts and militancy), became responsible for industrial liaison. Unlike the trade union official, away from the job, elected to office by people who did not know him or by a minority consisting of regular attendees at branch meetings, usually the politically committed, and by now as remote from his former workmates as the factory inspector, the shop steward was directly responsible to the men on the shop floor.

It was automatic that decisions had to be referred to each mass meeting, and the shop steward had to follow general decisions or re-sign his post. To the press, always seeking for "leaders" in order to personalize news stories, he was the "trouble-maker." So he was to the police, seeking a few scapegoats "in order to encourage the others." But the truth was that in an atmosphere of independence and con-scious militancy, such as already existed on Clydeside and which later spread—both here and in Germany—he was only the mouthpiece for the whole body of "trouble-makers." That is not to say that in some places, where there was a "committed" minority, the more persuasive speakers did not become shop stewards and effectual leaders of the movement. Ultimately, under the influence of the Russian Revolution, this happened almost everywhere. Leadership is sometimes inevitable, and something to which, in default of independent action, the liber-tarian revolutionary must be drawn or must abdicate action.

To speak of leadership is not necessarily to speak in authoritarian terms. It reflects not on the leaders so much as on the lack of spirit of the led. Free men need no leaders. Leadership may happen in default of spontaneity. It may be necessary to wake people up. It is still a fact that it affords too many temptations for the leadership to exercise au-thority and for it to step from delegatory mandatory office to making decisions for others. The *quality* of leadership at different periods is often criticized. What is wrong is the fact of leadership, and more particularly the necessity of it.

The linking-up of the shop-steward movement was firstly on the basis of mandating delegates, subject to recall. Only later did some of the more militant of these pass upwards into the role of leaders. The movement spread from factory to factory in British industry during the First World War. It began in the Scottish heavy industries and finally engulfed production, despite the eloquent appeals of Lloyd George and his kept union officials.[6] The proudest banner it had was the principle of workers' control, introduced by pre-war syndicalism, and in the course of its strategy it showed how workers' control could be achieved.

In Coventry, the *gang system* first reached the point of actual participation in management, beyond which workers' control could not go under capitalism without expropriation. The danger in the gang system is the very success it has since attained, for participation (with which the radical bourgeois economists of today have only just caught up) means a form of collaboration with the management which remains in office and is still answerable only to shareholders or directors (or, under nationalization, to the Board). In this situation the workers' movement degenerates to becoming a labor contractor. The gang system, the highest point that industrial democracy can reach, has many immediate material advantages, provided it is not confused with social change itself. Participation can only go so far. It is naturally confined to that which is held to concern labor. The bite at the cherry is in relation to the size of the cherry. It becomes in the interests of labor to pick larger cherries. Labor relieves management of the task of labor problems.

This last aspect has intrigued modern economists as the way of "solving social strife" which it may do within the factory "so long as it lasts," but it provides no means of solving social or economic problems other than the conditions of work or the size of the wage packet, important as these are under capitalism. The fluctuation of demand, bringing redundancy (which in itself proves the gang system is not workers' control) among other social problems, cannot be affected by it.

This of course does not displease those concerned from above with industrial relationships, consisting as they do of those who will form the new mandarin class. Social legislation for the control of industry is for the mandarins. Leave to the local council or to Parliament or to your trade union representatives the affairs that "concern the nation." In other words, leave it to us, the mandarins; you are already privileged beyond others in the degree of participation in your own working life. You have an interest in higher productivity and greater efficiency, which is all that counts under capitalism or state control.

This is what workers' control has come to mean in Yugoslavia today, and is advocated in this form by some in this country, including the "New Left" outside industry. They think it practical to urge the nationalization of industry, which is the State takeover of directorial boards and admittedly eliminates private profit, but substitutes a salariat in power. They modify nationalization with workers' control—in other words, allow in the State-run industry some participation in the actual running of work. To each his own: the mandarin has his responsibility, the worker has his.

This is a far cry from the idea of *direct* workers' control that arose in the shop stewards' movement half-a-century ago. The council communist movement of Germany at that period saw the dangers much more clearly than do the alleged admirers of Rosa Luxemburg (xxvi) now. Though regarded by many international socialists as the prophet of revolutionary socialism, her achievement was in the struggle against militarism (rare among the German socialists of the day) rather than as an industrial organizer, something for which, as a professional party "intellectual" she was scarcely fitted. Nor was she a theorist of the Spartacist movement as such except that she was the apologist within world communism for its ideas of workers' committees, as opposed to Lenin's fight for the party supreme.

The German Spartacist movement comprised at first the committees of industrial workers who had set up their network of delegates elected at the places of work, after the centralized trade unions had been absorbed in the war effort, in what was later seen to be a dress rehearsal for Nazism and the labor front less than twenty years later. Had the revolutionary movement not been shot down by democracy, democracy would not in turn have perished. The initial stages of revolution were successful everywhere. The floodgates of anarchy had been opened. The German fleet mutinied and the seamen set up their councils, not with the intention of improving their living standards within the Destruction State, but of achieving the social revolution.[7]

The sailors' councils were formed not just for the purpose of alleviating naval discipline, but for seizing the ships and ending the war. Councils spread like wildfire in the army, and the factory workers, asserting their strength, built up independent factory councils. The armed forces were sick of war and the industrial workers had prepared for revolution. The Kaiser always claimed in later years, as an exile in Holland, that his long life was due to his vigorous manual activity in chopping down the trees at Doom. One may take as more correct the expressed belief of one journalist that it was due to a good fast car ride out of Berlin.

The revolution in Russia had preceded the German Revolution, and the overthrow of Czarism and the establishment of "soviets" of workers, soldiers and peasants had inspired the revolutionary movement all over the world. It hastened the collapse of the war efforts in both Russia and Germany. The agent of the German general staff, financier, and socialist theorist (friend of Luxemburg and Trotsky), Helphand-Parvus, had foreseen the collapse of the Russian front if Lenin returned. Under his notorious arrangement with the imperial authorities, Lenin was sent back in the "sealed train" and supplied with German money. He did not overthrow the Czar. He overthrew the workers' councils.

Able to pay Lettish mercenaries to act as police, the Bolshevik faction was in a superior position from the first arrival of its leadership. They made a revolutionary appeal to the masses which became more persuasive when their left critics, whether social-revolutionary (xxvii), Menshevik social democrat, or anarchist, were removed by armed force. The most eloquent of opponents can be silenced by bullets or prison walls. The only effective answer to this was that of Dora Kaplan. A social-revolutionary, she attempted to assassinate Lenin.

The main struggle in the Russian labor movement became the attempt of the factory delegates to maintain independence. They tried to maintain at least a minimum of industrial democracy, against the encroaching demands of the party to be their "representative." Finally the party, by the legislation of trade unions, managed to incorporate them in the State machine, and so suppress opposition. This is something later imitated by the fascistic "corporate state" with employers' and workers' unions, and in our own time urged by the British Labor government. Those who have power to give have also the power to take away. The conferring of reality is a means of taking control. In Russia, the soviets became locals of the party, subordinate to the needs of the bureaucracy. The labor, productivity and welfare departments of the bureaucracy incorporated trade unionism, until finally the party and civil service formed part of a new ruling class.

However, the form of soviets and the creation of industrial democracy as a first step became a feature of all subsequent revolts in Russia and its satellites. In particular, the Hungarian Revolution of 1956 was an exercise in workers' councils, as a means of rising against the Russian-dominated civil service and police.[8] In China, and also in Yugoslavia, some form of industrial democracy was achieved. The workers participated in regulating their own working conditions, which some sociologists regard as the big deal, but they continued to be excluded from the control of economy. Management from outside, in this case by the party, continued to exist. They had a form of workers' control but under nationalization. The State had become the "neutral arbiter" between both sides of industry, and equally the appointments bureau for the management side and the electoral agent for the trade union side. In practice this meant a clash between the workers' committees and the State, management and party combined. In the great rebellions of China since Mao Tse-tung took power, the workers have clashed with the State directly, and the struggle against state communism has begun which has not yet been resolved.[9]

The Chinese anarchists of the early 1960s went forward from the idea of industrial democracy and sought direct workers' councils and the expropriation of industry from the State itself. Their struggle was similar to that of the German council communists fighting against capitalism. Only with the next stage, not yet reached in practice, can the difference between anarcho-syndicalism and council communism be shown. Both believe in forming committees at the places of work. Council communism limits the membership of such councils to delegates subject to recall. Anarchism would extend them from those chosen by their workmates, to everyone on the job. If this leads to decentralization and smaller units, even craft units, so let it be.

The anarchist movement within industry, in various countries however it might be labeled anarcho-syndicalist, rarely failed to see the essential difference between anarchism and revolutionary syndicalism, if only in order that the aims of the former should clarify the action to be taken by the latter. In cases where it failed to comprehend this, it ceased to be anarchist at all, and passed into the hands of socialists or parliamentarians, whose eloquence and outside organization, or use of police by legislation, ensured their success. The term "anarcho-syndicalist" arose not to channel off anarchism into the economic issues of the day, but to make industrial action effective and to bypass the State. It is a term that distinguishes between itself and the revolutionary syndicalism that parallels council communism. It also distinguishes itself from reformist syndicalism or from orthodox trade unionism in which revolutionaries might participate, the inadequacies of which activity have been criticized by Malatesta (xxviii), though he recognized its inevitability in some circumstances.

Revolutionary syndicalism accepts the idea of expropriation of the economic system, and the final aim of control by committees at the places of work, as against parliamentary reform or nationalization. Anarcho-syndicalism, agreeing with this, has gone further, to the idea of full participation by all within a free communistic society.

The use of the term *communism* implied that the basic unit of society should be the *commune*, the local community in which all forms of social and economic life should merge. In this sense, communism did not just hark back to the Paris Commune of 1870, as Lenin did when he abandoned the use of the name social-democrat because of its pro-war connotations. Free communism is an idea alien to the Communist Party.

A liberal criticism of free communism has been expressed as being that "everyone would be going backwards and forwards in committees to make sure agreements were generally in common." Liberalism by definition does not see farther than accepted capitalist values. The purpose of endless committee meetings, which might well be a feature of a decentralized labor movement, is to gain control. While the economic pressures of capitalism are on, the system needs to be sabotaged. In a free society itself, the need for constant reference-back becomes less. People doing a job in which they are interested have less need of committee discussion. No doubt the doctor refers to his hospital committees, but he does not refer back before every operation. He is independent in his own sphere. The worker can attain equal independence. It is for this reason, perhaps, that anarchist-communism generally appeared more feasible where there was an independent peasantry, or a working class at one remove from the peasantry.

It is true that Marxism in our time has flourished in the peasant countries, like Russia and China, and in the "colonial" lands more in deployment of military strategy than through any sympathy with the peasants as such. With the Che Guevara cult, it almost reverts to the ideas of the social-revolutionaries of Russia, and the guerrilla warfare appropriate to a peasant country is seen as a universally valid conception equally applicable to the campus of Bonn or the maquis hinterland of Christ's Pieces in Cambridge.

Classical Marxism, however, regards the peasantry as a feudal survival in capitalism, just as the small shopkeeper is considered a medieval survival in a monopoly society. The Russian social-revolutionaries looked on the peasantry as *the* class of social revolution, just as social democracy did the proletariat. Neither of these conceptions was anarchistic, but an independent peasantry could dispense with authority. So too could a freely organized commune, whether in city or country, as opposed to the commune collectivized from above.

The Israeli kibbutz is an example of a freely organized commune, though composed of settlers with authoritarian attitudes of one sort or another. It could not be called authoritarian communism, since that term has become so debased by its nominal association with state communism as to be totally misleading. Libertarian communes based upon consciously libertarian attitudes could have been seen on the opposite side of the Mediterranean, in the achievements of Catalonia during the Spanish Civil War. These attitudes have been implanted by Spanish anarchism over many years, and time and again, when it was a choice of starvation or hopeless rebellion, the peasants chose the latter and established the free commune, knowing the army (monarchist, republican, or fascist) would suppress it, but preferring to go down fighting.[10]

When, in 1936, the landlords fled, the way was open to free collectivization in Spain. It was a political need for Soviet imperialism to break up the Revolution, by making the Communist Party strong enough to do it. It was also fear of example, for they dreaded comparison of free communism with their own.

It was not the peasantry that gave birth to modern anarchism, though many peasant movements, especially that of Nestor Makhno (xxix) have tended that way. But it was certainly "the peasantry at one remove," the independent artisan or craftsman threatened as a class, and finally displaced as a viable section of society by the later monopolistic developments of capitalism. As an independent and productive class it had always been in the forefront of resistance against oppression because it neither stood in line for State benefits nor needed to beg for employment from masters. When State restrictions could be bypassed it did not even have to avail itself of the paper wealth of finance capital. It had been in the radical vanguard to destroy oppressive feudalism and often remained so, in the countryside. The "atheist blacksmith" or the "radical cobbler" were traditional "village Hampdens," rallying the village laborers, less able to express their opinions freely, to withstand the local gentry or clergy. Not entirely in derision, Marx called this class "petit bourgeois." It constituted the decentralizing federalists within the International, and is the reason why Marxists call anarchism a "petit-bourgeois trend" even today, when the term has come to mean something entirely different.

In its original sense, the "small citizens" were the backbone of the Paris Commune. French industry was still in the one-man stage and was threatened, under Napoleon III, by the fluctuations of exchange by which he planned to enable finance capital to grow, and to strengthen his empire's war potential. In consequence of the collapse both of France itself and of their means of livelihood, they established the Paris Commune. It was the high-water mark of Proudhonist decentralization.

In practice it began to merge with the stateless socialism advocated by the Bakuninist wing of the International. After the Commune was crushed, the amalgam of these ideas reverberated around the world. This was the birth of the modern anarchist movement proper.[11]

The master craftsman, small tradesman—cobbler, bookbinder, smith—who was the typical "small citizen" of this older economy, might sometimes have utilized an apprentice. He might have gone on to employ labor, expanded and become an exploiter. But while he remained an independent unit he was still a productive worker. As the history of the tailoring industry in this country demonstrates quite clearly, the smaller the degree of the employing unit, the greater the degree of exploitation. There is however a world of difference between the old-time craftsman as an independent man, and the master tailor who might originally be a craftsman, but whom the system obliged to go downwards to serve in a factory or upwards to become a capitalist himself. In the same way, a peasant might also become a large farmer, unless, as happened in most countries with an independent peasantry, the State, on behalf of the landowners, forcibly prevented him from doing so. The capitalist dilemma is expand or perish. This is why the petit bourgeoisie has become an exploiting class, but it has nothing in common with the older class given that name by Marx. Indeed the term now even includes the civil servant.

In the earlier, Proudhonian sense, it was possible to conceive of a libertarian society on the basis of the independent craftsman, on the lines of the medieval city. The decentralization of industry, once the workers came to control their own destinies in the form of guild socialism, might make such a vision a reality. The concept of independent craftsmen in guilds, and cooperative associations, was expounded scientifically by Kropotkin, and described lovingly by William Morris (xxx). It has never been far from the anarchist-communist view of utopia, whereas classical Marxism saw no farther than a successful proletariat controlling industry even where it realized that party control, and the very existence of a State machine, was destructive of that aim. To it the anarchist utopia was a "petty bourgeois" illusion, a term become the more insulting now that it has altered its meaning.

For today the term could never signify bakers or compositors or wheelwrights working on their own. Some of the old crafts have disappeared anyway, a change not always for the better.[12] Processes are now industrialized and the ruling motive is profit, not pleasure in craftsmanship. The individualist who does not have the luck or possess the ruthlessness to become an efficient businessman, is driven into mass industry or remains on the very edge of the economy.

In civil-service-controlled Russia, the stallholder is a despised substratum, generally someone who has "gone down in life" by being a rebel (by nature if not by politics) and has lost his all-important "papers"—his party card or his permit to work, miscalled a union card. He has "degenerated" to become a fruiterer or peddler. In this country, the costermonger, newspaper seller, taxi driver, all represent a hardy social tradition of the "tradesman." In the older, Proudhonian sense, they are "bourgeois." They are unmistakably working-class in the social sense.

The gauche mistranslation—"petty bourgeois" (*petit bourgeois, Kleinbürger*, small citizen)—has caught on because it is apt enough to describe this class in its new sense. For its most noticeable feature is its pettiness. In general jargon the term is applied to the city businessman, the civil servant, the multiple shopkeeper, the professional man or woman, the office executive. The socially petty-minded, irrespective of occupation, regard themselves as middle-class. The smaller shopkeeper's aspirations make an attractive archetypal myth ("the small man") for the Beaverbrook Press. It conceals the reality that capitalism has reduced him to the status of an outworking contractor in those trades where there is insufficient incentive for employees. That is why the side street grocer gives way to the supermarket, whose cut-down of labor makes retail trading profitable.

There is still a place in the rat-race for the tobacconist prepared to stand in a kiosk for all hours of the day, smiling at his civil service customers in bowler hat and striped trousers, perhaps thinking of himself as middle-class and of them as office workers, while they regard themselves as middle-class and him as a tradesman. His takings siphoned off to the State by way of tax and to the manufacturer and wholesaler by way of profit, his margin is barely viable to allow the payment of wages, which is why the distributive end was left to him in the first place. Providing he introduces sufficient capital, it may return to him by installments without his realizing the nature of the con game, or he may attribute the slowness of re-accumulation to the faults of the current government or possibly to the unofficial strikers or even the long hair of modern youth.

This represents the antithesis of the independence to which he lays claim. It is a form of liberty without cooperation which finally ceases to be liberty. Freedom is not possible without cooperation. Cooperation without freedom is another form of exploitation.

Social Protest and a New Class

THE APPALLING PROGRESS AND prospects of the Destruction State, the increased powerlessness of the individual, and the increased meaninglessness of party or established beliefs held all over the world, gave an enormous impetus to social protest. It was a secular revolution against the neo-Churches. It began on well-worn, anti-militarist lines, if with some imaginative overtones, but nevertheless tended to follow certain patterns of the class struggle. This was against the expectations of some of those who, like many radical leaders, think that to run a little ahead of the crowd is to lead it.

The general climate of social protest was a revival of militant liberalism. Political liberalism was institutionalized and dead, and in the new form the old radicalism walked again on earth. It developed ideas and gimmicks anticipated even by the suffragettes but moved further on in face of the accepted irrelevance of protest as such. Protest had become a ritual part of the scene, officially tolerated and even encouraged within limits. But when it had gone beyond those limits, police defense of the status quo, in some countries reaching the point of brutal social conquest, which is the nature of the State, had sharpened the teeth of protest. The Dutch Provos, perceiving this, had the idea of deliberately provoking the State to do so and show its true nature.

It was natural that anarchists would be among those militant in the protest movement, since demonstrations on the streets against the State, like strike action, must weaken the sequence of command-and-obey. It would not have been illogical for the revolutionary anarchist otherwise to have taken the stand of a few sectarian Marxists who stated that such a movement was irrelevant to social change and should be ignored. As it happened, the anarchists were usually the main targets for police attack because they included the most militant protesters, and conversely, the anarchist banners rallied the most militant protesters because there the police attack would be strongest. So anarchism has appeared to many, solely on the street level without consideration of other factors, the most aggressive form of dissension. This might be so, but the conclusion, that the most aggressive form of dissension must therefore be anarchism, was quite false, though it was assumed to be true by many going forward from CND (xxxi).

Hence the confusion, amusing or irritating to the revolutionary anarchist according to temperament, that militant liberalism and anarchism are the same thing. The former sometimes assumes the name of anarchism, at least with the dilutive hyphenation "pacifist-anarchism." That is not to say that a person professing the pacifist creed could not be an anarchist, or vice versa;[12] but the hybrid, pacifist-anarchism, certainly as expounded by the fakirs of Peace News, is so patently militant liberalism as to make it difficult for Young Liberals to tell the difference.

Perhaps militant liberalism may be included under the umbrella of the libertarian movement. The definition has become somewhat wide in the last few years. It is an abuse of words, however, to call it anarchist, however it may label itself. It cannot comprehend a means of social change, short of an appeal to the rich to give up their possessions, as advocated by Vinoba Bhave and the Gramdan movement in India and lauded by the orthodox peace movement. Even those who believe in many-handed gods and are afraid when the lizard croaks find it hard to believe this is possible.

The limitations of the protest movement, and of all militant liberalism however radical and libertarian it might become and however advanced it has developed in the United States, rest on its inability to comprehend the class struggle, without the recognition of which social change is not possible. It may try to justify itself by criticizing "outmoded conceptions" which were never in mode except by way of hyperbole rather than analysis (for instance, by denouncing the Kingsleyan-type messianism and attributing it to "Marx and Bakunin").

This advanced liberal thesis, masquerading as pacifist-anarchism, has attracted a substantial section of a generation of radicals. And further, in Hegelian terms, this thesis put forward by those coming from a middle-class background, has confronted its antithesis, the "fascism" of their parents which springs from a paranoiac fear of state communism. This basic fascism, of the primitive Mussolinian type, is a sort of homeopathic remedy for state communism, which leads them to advocate its measures.

Thesis and antithesis call into being a synthesis which is seen in the "situationist" movement in particular, and in the hippie movement and variations upon its theme. Understanding this enables us to dispense with reliance on the "generation gap" beloved by journalists. In the various splits and counter-splits of, the situationists, in the American-inspired hippie movement, the old jazz-'n'-drugs scene, the International Times and its esoteric successors and competitors, the antithesis is worked out. There is a contempt for the "masses"—"Alfs" is the word given by the magazine "Oz"—for the squares, prollies, lumps—mingled with peace-movement gimmicks to wake up the bourgeoisie (but directed at them all the same). The vanguard of social progress becomes educated youth, the students, the "provotariat." The natural elite of society is "the beautiful people." Society is despised for itself and not for its accepted values. There is a cult of death, manifest in an addiction for the hard stuff and in the way such movements move on to Eastern mysticism and the cults that produce Books of the Dead. The way to change society is to go off on trips to the astral plane by way of narcotics, so that everything becomes ideal while remaining exactly the same (liberal reformism in a new guise?).

Alternatively, though in essence similarly, there is the idea of self-responsibility, the pretensions to curb individual aggressiveness, or the creation of outlets for frustrated youth to enable it to adjust to society. Voluntary social welfare is taken to be social revolution. Do-goodism adopts a swinging image—first-aid for junkies, meth-drinkers and vagrants—and inspires, for instance, the "Catholic Worker" movement with its Romanist charity obsession (that was guyed in Buñuel's *Viridiana*), with the tramp-glorification of American individualism ("Hallelujah, I'm a bum!") and this has gone round the scene in various guises.

Nevertheless, this is not to criticize any or all of these too severely, at least not as long as they understand their unimportance (which so few of us do). It is certainly not to join in the petty bourgeois disapproval of them for their shock value. Anything will shock the petty-minded, from a variation in hairstyles to the use of narcotics not hallowed by commercial exploitation nor legal sanction.

"Dropping out," the slogan of the hippie movement, is fine, whether one thinks of it as ignoring the rat race, or in terms of a community of neo-Diggers, utopian socialists, or saints in a cooperative farm; or, for a sufficiently well-heeled Thoreau (xxxiii), in the rustic delights of a cottage by Walden Pond. The weekend hippie, who drops out when he is not working in the bank, is no more to be derided than the vacation yachtsman, a son of the sea when he is not calculating actuarial statistics on life expectancy.

There have been some well-intentioned radicals who have told us that if we wish neither to be exploited nor to exploit others, we should be window-cleaners or sell hot dogs. The point of view is a vocational hazard of individualism. It is an idealisation, such as it is, of what happens to the formerly independent craftsman. People with the cash availability may equally think in terms of owning their own desert island and getting away from the wicked world. It is all very true but has nothing to do with social change which is dependent upon economic liberation.

If national liberation has been said to be a good breakfast but a poor supper, militant liberalism is a good mid-morning snack and may even, if we are not too demanding, serve as the midday meal itself; it cannot last us until evening.

The new liberalism has not remained still. A large part of the "elite" dissatisfied with its inadequacies, has adapted it to greater militancy. In some cases they have gone on to revive the theories of Blanqui or make a cult of Che Guevara. It is, however, only the press, invariably less informed than the public it serves, which sees the protest movement solely comprised of students, and the university composed of the "New Left." The industrial worker lags in his support of this New Left because he sees it in terms of the old liberalism writ large. It is not untrue that he is more inclined to be conservative in his manner of thinking when he is not directly relating it to his own experiences. The new radical student may get infuriated when the industrial worker distrusts him, recalling the student of 1926, as if the students who helped to break the strike then were not now nearing retirement age, and were then, in any case, very different in social origin and outlook from those of the present time. But university radicalism, like artist bohemianism, may for some be fashionable and harmless, even possibly useful to a future career. It is another matter to be blacklisted in the only trade to which one's apprenticeship applies.

It is for this reason that those most active in defiance of the State have become, except on purely industrial issues, those most divorced from productive work, yet remaining socially of the lower class rather than the upper and certainly having no responsibility for the domination of society. They may be working in driving jobs, offices, shops or other peripheral trades. They may have come through the universities. They are often the end-product of sausage-factory grammar-school education. They have in common the fact that they can chop and change around so far as employment is concerned, admittedly not always to their financial benefit. They can, however, be reasonably independent of induced public opinion, certainly until family responsibilities overtake social commitments and force a surrender to the conformity of the petty-minded.

Here we see a new class in the making. In one sense it is independent, and though in times of depression it is disastrous to lose jobs, yet at other times it does not really matter two hoots to people in this class whether they have one job or another. A clerk, for example, may jump from the wine trade to the post office and finish up exporting dry goods, with all the careless abandon of a cabinet minister swapping portfolios.

The not unnatural, if commercially unjustifiable, desire of business executives to have pretty girls showing their legs around the office has led to higher wages (which the "could never afford" for a nurse or factory girl) being offered to younger shorthand-typists and secretaries. This has been enhanced by the free use of the individual strike, flitting from job to job, which has put up salaries still more, though many of the girls concerned might shake their heads sadly at the thought of other peoples strike action, which everybody knows is the reason "the country" is going to the dogs.

Despite all this apparent independence, the class to which we are referring is still helpless as far as social affairs are concerned and alienated from any voice in political matters or economic betterment. It can only "trust the government," and the clerk tends to blame his problems upon whatever politician happens to be in office at the moment, if not upon the trade unions or the financiers according to ideology. The park keeper and meter reader, who do not usually identify themselves with the middle class, out of social prejudice, are in a similar position. They do not have the productive power of the aeroplane engineer, for instance, although their degree of social usefulness might be higher or might be lower.

Unless such workers happen to work in large numbers (dustmen or postmen for example), their power to strike is diminished, and the conception of the struggle becomes more nebulous for them than it does for those on the factory floor. Indeed, it often appears that the more socially useful a job is, the more difficult it is to perceive that there is in fact a class struggle. It is easy to see that there are two sides in a car plant, less easy to see a division of interest on a farm, and almost impossible to understand it working in a hospital. Because of this, the conception of workers' control becomes less clearly understood where there is at a given moment a shared interest in a job. A commercial traveler, working upon commission, could only discover the nature of the struggle by his reading or understanding and might conclude it was an academic conception.

What distinguishes this class, consisting of varied occupations and degrees of prosperity, which gets bigger while the industrial class gets smaller? It is the fact of dispossession of a class from all productive work that is not marginal to the economy.

Is there a precedent? Nineteenth-century capitalism developed a class that consisted of the permanently unemployed, and of the "rogues and vagabonds" of feudalism, as well as of those evicted from the land. It was swelled by workers dispossessed by machinery, by unmoneyed idlers, lazy out of their appropriate class, and, by those who struggled for general laboring jobs at the bottom of the social ladder. It included the peddler, the beggar, the petty criminal. Marx labeled this class, somewhat condescendingly, the "lumpenproletariat," the rogue workers. It was the substratum, seen in the "children of the Jago," the London of Dickens and Mayhew, the "submerged tenth," the "people of the abyss," those in "darkest England." Perhaps it is seen in the worse American Negro "ghettos" of today.

It is a productive class deliberately made unproductive for the most part, and productive only by accident. It has been referred to by some sociologists as the "Lazarus class."

By a similar exegesis we may refer to the other, newer class deprived of its productive ability, though not in this case its capacity to work, as the "Naboth class." The vineyard of which it has been dispossessed is that of independent productiveness. Unlike the Lazarus class, it is not dependent on the rich man's (in practice, more often the poor man's) table for crumbs. On the contrary, even without the vineyard it remains a useful part of society, though the least useful the tasks it undertakes, the more commercially rewarding they appear to be.

In the mighty office blocks towering to the glory of our modern checkbook Caesars, tribute to the mighty is counted not by the centurions at their command but by the number of staff beneath them. However poky or inadequate the factory might be that produces the wealth on which the office block subsists, if indeed the whole edifice does not deal in invisibility, the prestige office soars to the heavens and those who produce its memos are better paid than those who produce its wealth.

What point is there in saying that most people probably enter the servitude of this class voluntarily? That applies to every class from the most submerged to the most oppressive except that most people prefer to go upwards rather than downwards. For years the grammar schools have churned out pupils in the sausage-machine of education, divorcing them from their social class but failing to give them the opportunity to escape from it economically. They left the humanistic cultures of the sixth form to fill up inkwells and write in ledgers or, in the case of girls, to learn shorthand at a hundred words per minute to take dictation from bosses who think at twenty words per minute. Only in the last few years has the wastage become apparent, and higher education open for less obviously time-filling jobs. The separation from social origins, however, remains the same.

In these circumstances some have come to think of themselves, contrary to all reason, as "middle-class," or at any rate "lower middle-class," when they are nothing of the sort. In the inter-war period, fascism made the most of its appeal to those who, thinking of themselves as "lower middle-class"—lower class economically, middle-class in aspiration, therefore felt a kinship to the dominant class that was not reciprocated except by way of idealisation (ex-service, comradeship, or fellow-membership of "the nation"). Reaction directed their sense of frustration at the nearest available scapegoat. They felt a vague resentment at being thought of as petty bourgeois, in the new insulting sense, by the socialist movement, and the face-saving definition of "workers by hand and brain" made no impression. (One may speculate on the interesting possibility of working without either or both, except in a government department or a factory for the handicapped.)

But while fascism out of power tried to make a bid to rally this emerging class, to give a larger base to an elitist movement, it had no role but demo-fodder for anyone not of the elite. It extended its bid, once in power, to include the industrial workers, and used the people as a whole as cannon-fodder. The Nazi philosophy embraced the notion of a civil war against the lower orders in order that a preordained ruling class might take power in the State. The master-race was seen as a ruling class *within* the nation. Only during the bid for popular support was the theory re-phrased in such a way that it might appear that the *nation* was regarded as being part of the master race.[13]

Once fascism got over the initial shock of putting the bully-boys of opposition into the halls of the mighty, it fitted comfortably into an administrative bureaucracy, exactly the feature of state communism that most repelled those to whom the fascist appealed. Even the mass-murder camps of Hitler's Germany were run by an established civil service that settled into a routine which, given time, might have introduced competitive examinations and birthday honors.

It was regarded as the major reform of fascism to "problem of unemployment" by taking workers evicted by the processes of capitalism from their capability of productiveness, and placing them at the service of the State. Instead of letting them filter into light or non-essential industry, which was the only alternative in a capitalist society to mass unemployment, it diluted private capitalism with state serfdom and made them serve the war machine or engage in pyramid-type achievements such as the autobahn.

Seen in this light, the concentration camps were not divergence from fascist ideas, as Bernard Shaw thought at the time and the apologists for Nazism have since proclaimed. They were primarily, of course, the means of inflicting terror, since the party, even before its accession to power, had picked on a scapegoat and isolated it as a smaller, distinct section. Its display of strength upon that minority, which fell back on constitutional protests and even appeals to conscience, never heeded in power politics, meant that it could isolate other sections and terrorize each of them in turn, too. This is normal street gang or police tactics and part of the technique of divide-and-conquer which leads to command-and-obey. In addition, however, the concentration camps were an essential part of the switch from capitalism to State control. Finally, even the great industrialists who had financed Hitler found themselves subordinate to the governmental complex, and the possession of wealth became less important than the right connections in a ministry. The existence of a terror machine was a gun pointed at the capitalist and the army officer no less than at the worker. Naturally it was possible to solve the unemployment problem if everyone had to work where they were told, at dictated conditions and wages.

The Soviet forced labor camps had the same political and economic aims. Russia, being tied to a non-competitive ideology, was slower to evict workers from productivity and to reduce them to State-fodder, in the same way as the capitalist countries did with their unemployed. Scarcity in any case meant that the country needed goods and was short of workers rather than otherwise. But for the State to exercise full control, it was essential that there be a pit into which the recalcitrant could fall. Since it was not the stagnation of unemployment amidst depression, it had to be taming the Siberian wilds. They did not require a totally non-productive class. Since the State was master, it might as well keep the "people of the abyss" building useless pyramids. Had there not been political offenders, it would have been necessary to invent them.

Totalitarianism is not bound by the new economics which teaches that labor is the most expensive item on the sheet, and the Russian commissars are therefore more inclined than otherwise to keep the socialist definition that labor is the measurement of everything. So the escapes by way of opting out of the system are closed, except for a few from the vanishing lumpenproletariat, who can carry on street trading for a time, and a few from the "intelligentsia," who will sing and paint the glories of the regime.

Even so, the tendencies towards a "Naboth class" are not entirely absent from Russia as the bureaucracy "liberalizes" economically, i.e. moves from state communism to state rule and so to state capitalism. The same conditions as in state capitalism are being created. The civil service needs its quota of clerks, counting its glory in the number of serfs at its disposal. The school conveyor-belts turn out students geared to serve the dictated needs of the bureaucracy. It is not surprising that rebellion begins to grow among the younger generation, which now realizes that this process is coming to be regarded as inevitable.

The capitalist is less inhibited than the Soviet commissar in feeling, or thinking that he ought to feel, that labor is the source of his power. On the contrary, he resents being dependent on the worker, and the new, literate generation of capitalists is inclined to throw back the charge. "You are the parasites on us!" is what in effect their political mouthpieces say to the productive worker, and the press expands on the theme, sometimes with more tact and sometimes with less. Labor is "expensive," it is capable of becoming "redundant," it ought to be more "mobile" It is the "dearest item of cost." Once the boss said, "We give you work." Now he is able to say, "We do not need you." Labor "fails to adapt itself to new methods"—so bring in the machinery, push out the men! The robots are taking over, the productive processes bring in—not Kropotkin's utopia, because it is not willed—but the anti-utopia of Aldous Huxley's *Brave New World* and George Orwell's *1984*.

Once labor ceases to be the vital element of society, there remains the problem of what to do with the displaced. One can leave the economy alone and create a vast class of unemployed. One can set out to create a lumpenproletariat. Alternatively it is possible to put labor into the side jobs of the economy. Creating unemployment, the first method, has been tried and found dangerous to the stability of the regime. It is even now advanced, at least in minor touches, by influential sections of the Conservative Party as the best way to flick the whip, but most moderate politicians are afraid that the beast will get out of control after the lashing. Creating a lumpenproletariat is seldom done deliberately by the State. When it is done irresponsibly by laissez-faire capitalists, it causes a bourgeois reaction to cheap government. They call for stronger rule, as in parts of the U.S. today. The most favored method now of dealing with displaced labor is to take it from being a class of producers and to make it a peripheral class. Shipyards are closed, but they cannot find enough doormen for the vast office blocks. University degrees are given in means of cutting down the number of workers employed in creative work, but there is an acute shortage of bookkeepers.

The moment one begins to consider staff shortages, the whole question of emigration and immigration arises. Changes in the economy are always accompanied by the shifting around of populations. It is part of the normal pattern of social conquest. The military subjugation of the Scottish Highlands was inseparable from the change in its way of life, and evicting the crofters was as much part of military conquest as it was of economic change. Emigration is the prophylactic of revolution, as seen clearly in Ireland even up to the present day. "Here or nowhere is your America," said Goethe. The French, said Heine somewhat too optimistically, do not emigrate; they stay where they are and let their tyrants emigrate—in short, they create a revolution.

It has suited the capitalist class to see huge numbers of workers go out, and in some cases be driven out, to create new markets in Australia, New Zealand, and Canada. It is both more bourgeois and more civilized than Russia's colonization of Siberia by prison labor, at least since deportations to Australia became obsolete. New markets for expansion are created in this way, and the home economy is transformed by getting rid of those whom it is no longer necessary to exploit.

The ruling class in the new countries tend to be more democratic in their habits than those in the older countries, but sooner rather than later a new moneyed aristocracy is recreated, and the gap between rulers and ruled made plain.

Emigration from one country means immigration into another, and normally immigration brings problems of adjustment, especially when the immigrant cannot hide his identity because of language, religion, or color. All the usual State ideology—"our country" as opposed to *theirs,* meaning *we* were the serfs of the government first—reacts against the immigrant even when not aggravated by living cheek-to-jowl in the slums with people of different customs or cookery. Only when immigration can be seen giving demonstrable benefits, whether real or imagined, does the established working class accept it, as in Israel. The ruling class will not accept it unless it brings practical benefits to them, chiefly by way of cheap or diluted labor, but not if it brings labor problems in its wake. One has only to examine the progress of the US immigration laws.

Opposition to immigration today has become in Britain a bandwagon on which discredited fascism has jumped. It is no accident that the section of the Conservative Party, exemplified by Enoch Powell, which advocates the touch of the whip by unemployment, also opposes immigration, at least to the extent of creating feeling against it. But they do not seriously intend to take positive action since the situation of having discontent suits them, and it would be fatal to dispense with a scapegoat. It is convenient for them to encourage emigration and to discourage immigration only to the point of creating dissension and so to "change the color" of the working class, as it were—to have the "troublesome" labor jobs, in transport for instance, filled by those who would be subject to discrimination and dislike not because they are workers but because they are racially distinguishable.

It is a sophisticated version of the Hindu caste system. It is not fascism, even though the adherents of the latter advocate it to save themselves from oblivion. The big fist against the workers is not required by capitalism, and men like Powell have learned that fascism is a two-edged weapon. The German capitalists found it was as much a boomerang as Ludendorff's "sealed train" strategy. In any case, the identification of fascism as such with a defeated imperialism makes it unable any more, of itself, to be a popular rallying point, which was its original attraction to the capitalists. The measures of the corporate, state have long since been adapted to democratic government by liberally educated economists to whom the brutality of Hitlerism has no attraction when not necessary. An argument over immigration, pro and con, may suit the political book, but fascism has become a gadfly. It has no relation to class issues, and so far as any effectiveness is concerned, joins the anti-vivisectionists or the militant teetotalers or the spiritualists as flies upon the wheel. Such movements are socially irrelevant. They may be good (anti-animal cruelty), bad (Scientology), or delightfully indifferent (Joanna Southcott's box). They may make an impact upon people's lives (Jehovah's Witnesses). It is, for instance, unpleasant to have a fascist group—irrespective of the fact that it is never likely to gain power-nagging away at one's color without even offering a helpful suggestion as to how to change it. But no such grouping can make any fundamental change in the community. This must have some connection with the relation of one class to another. If we all joined the Lord's Day Observance Society, we would be in for some dreary Scottish-type Sundays, but a change in the structure of the economy would not be effected by Sabbatarianism.

It may well be asked if the libertarian can make an impact upon society, or if he is doomed to be lumped with the advocates of funny money or pure water. This was certainly the case in the 1920s when the issue of free decentralization seemed as irrelevant to the changing pattern of society as the preservation of the waterways. But it cannot be said now. The industrial worker has to choose between taking over society or disappearing as a productive class. The Fabians were right when they predicted that "the working class would disappear." But they did not imply that we should all become film stars or advertising executives or chairmen of companies. Those occupations are the wrappings around the monolithic State. When the "working class disappears" it will be a major disaster like the dispossession of the peasantry.

It is happening slowly, but it is implicit in the patterns of today. For this reason any protest movement arising even out of a purely negative character, hostile reaction to mass annihilation, comes to be identified generally with resistance to the Destruction State, whether passively or actively. From it has come a movement of spontaneous revolution that is spreading across the world. If mankind survives the State, the academic and journalistic illusion that this movement is only a manifestation of youthful high spirits will be laughed at by history.

Do Classes Exist?

DO THE CLASSES OF WHICH we are speaking really exist? Is it all only based on illusion? Have the mass media finally persuaded us that it is all "Marxist jargon" and that we are all workers now, because Lady Mary spends her days in a boutique and the Earl himself has to show visitors around his stately mansion?

There is so much confusion that we have not only to spell out what is meant by "classes," but to explain it by diagrams.

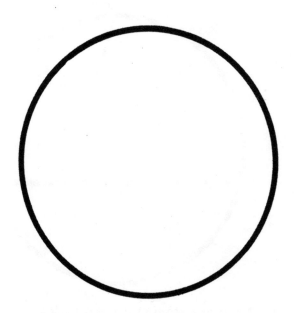

fig.1 early society

Society is represented by a circle, and the primitive society (fig. 1) is an empty circle. There are neither State organs nor classes. It might have a titular chief, but if we represent him by a point on the circumference, it means nothing whatsoever until (fig. 2) he has created some form of repressive machinery. When the slave-driver has cracked his whip, the first dominant class appears; the free men of the tribe as against the slaves. Together with the warriors they are the first force that can be used for internal oppression as well as external aggression or defense.

In the medieval society (fig. 3) we can see that the ruling class has begun to emerge.

It forms the upper strata, with the Church as a cross-segment. In some societies the "armed forces" segment can be extended to include the rest of the circle (for all men are warriors). In some, the Church has to be extended, for all are "believers." But even so, there emerges the division of rule in the form of judicature and legislature, and the enforcement of decisions made by the upper strata separates off the lower horizontal strata, until modem capitalistic society emerges (fig. 4).

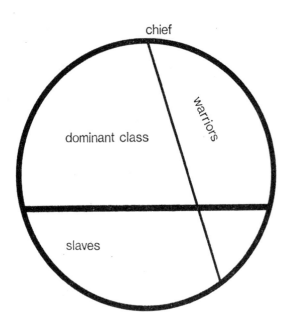

fig.2 the primitive state

In the top segment of capitalistic society is the "gilded amalgam" of landowners, industrialists, financiers, bankers. The top section cuts across the vertical divisions, and marks out the generals, leading industrialists, top civil servants, judges, and so on. But it is firmly divided horizontally from the rest of society.

It is not all but impossible to pass over that firm line as it was in feudal society when only the Church provided a bridge. Victorian and Edwardian novels are full of the dilemmas of those who do pass over the line. There have been self-made millionaires and ambitious politicians. But all the same, there is at all times—so far as this firm line is concerned—a clear distinction as to who is "above" and who is "below," even under a democratic process of election to some of the right-hand sections.

The middle class is divided in our diagram from the working class by a wavy line. Not firm, it goes up and down like a Geiger counter (fig. 5).

The so called "lower middle class" can be down on "working-class" levels, such as those for instance in clerical occupations who, as

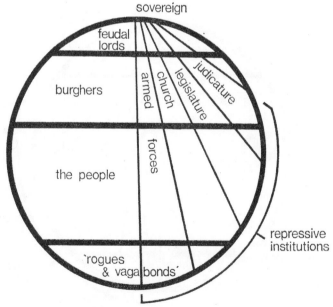

fig.3 medieval society

a result of snobbery or establishment propaganda, imagine themselves to be bourgeois, or are treated as such socially without being so economically. There may be shopkeepers, after bankruptcy say, or market stallholders, who, according to economists, would be "middle-class" but might reach down into the submerged level.

The existence of this submerged level is a repressive force just as much as are the armed or police forces. The fear of falling into the pit may be greater than the threat of imprisonment. Criminals certainly have found this to be the case. The submerged level may rise in times of depression. It may even take in what we might call the bottom of the civil service, people employed by the State on road duties, public works, and even conscript soldiers at the old penny-a-day level.

In the middle-class horizontal level, on the right-hand side, we find chief constables, bank managers, trade union leaders. On the same side of the working-class stratum, we find policemen. A hoary question asked of the libertarian revolutionary is whether he considers policemen workers? Clearly yes, but in the right-hand segment. Their economic interests are the same, but they are still divided by

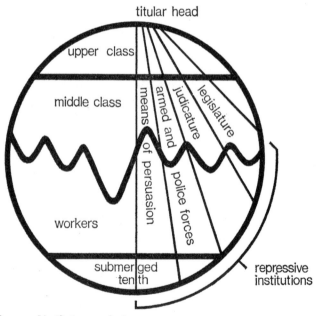

fig.4 capitalist society

the governmental system (vertical line) though not by the horizontal (class) one. In this case, ideas of duty make the line impassable. The soldier, especially if a conscript, may ignore the line when the sequence of command-and-obey is broken. Even the police have done so (the police strike) but normally when they do so they are dismissed and cease to be policemen.

The strengthening of the police role, because of the difficulties in the enforcement of government, may lead to a police state. But this does not have any effect upon the social economic structure of society under the State other than one of maintaining domination. It is not in their reliance upon the police that state communism and fascism differ from democracies, which may also move to a police state (the U.S. has done so more than once). In the totalitarian system (fig. 6) the civil service includes the whole circle; sooner or later everyone becomes a servant of the State.

Under state socialism or communism, the class divisions (straight and wavy lines) become obliterated and may even ultimately disappear. Not so in fascism. But in both, the ruling class tends to become identified

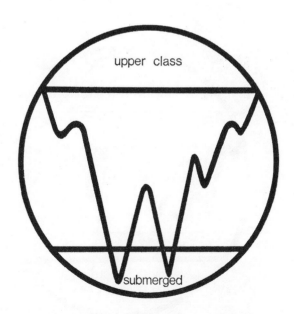

fig.5 the ʿgeiger–counterʾ of capitalism

with that part of the vertical segments labeled "the bureaucracy," which has taken the older role of the Church. The horizontal layer at the bottom does not disappear. Even if it should come to be no longer required by economic necessity, because artificial "depressions" are cured, it is essential to have a limbo to which prisoners of war, political prisoners, forced labor, penal battalions, and the like can be consigned.

The tendency of the party, if the totalitarian regime moves on and is not cut short in its prime, is to stabilize the circle with an inner segment (fig. 7).

The head of state is supreme. If classes still exist, it includes a mixture of them. The bureaucracy, though nominally party members, are outside any control by it. The submerged level includes those who have lost their party cards and may even rise to include the lower ranks of the party (the deviationists).

It is true that the divisions are not so clear in reality as they are in our diagrams. The art of establishment and party propaganda alike is to blur the fact that there are such divisions. Because it is on occasion possible to ignore them, and sometimes to be genuinely unaware of

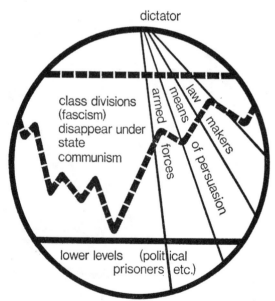

fig.6 the totalitarian state

their existence, it is assumed that they do not exist. A self-employed newspaper seller may harbor the illusion that he has more in common with the directors of W.H. Smith & Sons than he has with the working class.

Laissez-faire capitalism would blur the segmentary lines. Social-democracy would revise them. In a welfare state, the Geiger line would vary and might even be regulated. Toryism would maintain the straight line. Kings and presidents are imaginary dots on the circle. Dictators maintain their power only when they can maintain their place on the circumference where lines of division meet. For power exists when the will of the people and the wishes of the rulers coincide. Fashioning the will of the people is the first essential of government.

The segments in these diagrams are not, of course, drawn proportionately. What the correct proportions should be is part of the stuff of political debate. Should we cut down on the civil service? Curb government spending? Disestablish the Church? Revise defense estimates? Extend the legal system? Where is the line between the classes to be drawn?

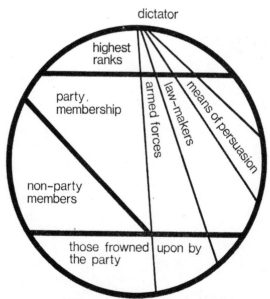

fig.7 the totalitarian party in society

By rejecting this debate, we are advocating the return to a blank circle. The free society would be differentiated from primitive society by its mode of production and its level of culture. Its lack of masters or repressive institutions would ensure that man "born free" would live free.

Reward and Fantasies

HISTORY EXCUSES ROBBERY AND the law sanctions it. Even though the thief himself may not die in the odor of sanctity, provided he holds sufficient loot intact to pass on to his descendants, the hereditary principle will provide that his grandchildren may grow up virtuously and live graciously. The rich can afford virtue; the poor may well practice it the more but can seldom afford it.

The descendants of the brigands who stole the land from the Scottish people are proud that their fathers fought for what they now possess, and are most indignant at the notion that they themselves may have to fight for it again. But the British landowning nobility as a whole is resigned to its present situation. They married—both literally and metaphorically—into the capitalist class and are also able to ensure their transition into the meritocracy. The Foreign Office, for instance, is traditionally "a form of outdoor relief for the aristocracy."

Even the Crown fancies its chances of survival as a harmless tourist attraction. But the very symbolism by which it justifies itself makes this an optimistic expectation to say the least, so far as a revolutionary Britain is concerned. By being over-plugged now it may not even stand a chance of a good engagement in Hollywood after its long run in London.

Is the monarchy a dead issue already? This is what the press would have us believe, damning the institution with faint praise. Involving the Crown "in politics" is the worst sin that a politician can commit, and his opponents fall over themselves trying to prove he did it. But since the Crown sets the seal of legality upon decisions which are made by the British State, it is more than the personality cult it appears to be. Republicanism is certainly a dead issue. It can make no appeal to the propertied. If the lands of the Crown are expropriated, what excuse is there for not seizing those of the aristocracy? And why should it end there?

This is the dilemma in which Scottish nationalism, like Welsh and Irish, finds itself. It either becomes another escape route into Parliament for yet another group of politicians, or it determines on a positive course of action which is inevitably republican. But if it does so, the propertied gentry who are its main protagonists on a cultural level sooner or later find themselves involved in a movement for social expropriation.[14] They have opened the floodgates of anarchy. The nationalist leaders, as in Ireland, are then said to "sell out," though one ought to give them credit for being consistent in defense of their own interests. If, at this point, they have to rely upon the troops of their former enemy, they will do so, though they naturally prefer to use their own. Anything is better than expropriation.

Why is expropriation essential to a social revolution? Could not the former "ruling class" be compensated? The answer has divided the "legitimate" socialist from the revolutionary. The former, at least until the possibility of the attainment of office made the whole question academic, always allowed that the nation should possess the land by which the community was held to ransom, and the means of production by which the capitalist was able to exploit those with only their labor to sell. The orthodox Marxist believed that the concentration of wealth under monopoly capitalism made its expropriation inevitable.

The parliamentary tendency of social-democracy agreed. "But let the expropriated class be compensated!" Why? In order to allow them to retain a privileged position? There is no compensation for power but power. To enable their power to be exchanged at a fair price into another currency, is to enable that currency to be exchanged back into power, even if at a small brokerage. Under state socialism with compensation, as under fascist state capitalism, or British democratic state socialism, the "expropriated" class would become the new "meritocracy." Merit, like virtue, is the adopted child of money. Naturally the package-deal of Fabianism (state socialism with compensation) has appealed to that section of the already "meritocratic" professional class with sufficient intelligence to perceive the inevitability of some sort of social change. It has even conquered the "pink" section of the Conservative Party, as distinct from and to the dismay of the American conservative.

What is the "merit" of the meritocracy? It is not the "merit" of courage or devotion or craft or industry, though it is quite conceivable that some of its members may possess a few or even all of these qualities. It is simply the ability to administer. It is the art of ruling, the transmitting of the line of command-and-obey. Merit in this sense is measured solely by its service to the State, and the degree by which the servant becomes the master. For this reason it appeals to the professional class; it is their own revolutionary class theory.

Fabianism involves the gradual permeation of these ideas. It is now the common property of many parties, but advances the interests of one section only, though it no doubt sincerely believes that the samurai in question will be the saviors of us all. Most of the reforms of the past forty years come back to the panacea of State intervention and the role of Big Brother. They all have a family likeness. The prototype was "putting the unemployed on public services," the daring social reform of the 1920s. "Reforms" of this nature foreshadow coming social changes. The "reformist" puts a liberal gloss on what is going to happen anyway.

Looking curiously at the yellowing party programs and their outworn slogans, one can see the Fabian touch not only in MacDonald's Labor Party, as well as Lansbury's, with touching faith in the nationalization of the mines and railways, for instance, but also in the old Independent Labor Party, both of Keir Hardie and of Maxton, which saw great things once dependence on the Liberals had been shaken. Even Trotsky believed that once British labor had got rid of MacDonald, Snowden, and Jimmy Thomas it would be on the high road to social revolution. Its ideas appeared advanced to those who saw the State as the measurement of man. On the right wing, there was the early Mosley and the middle-period Macmillan, flogging the public works theme, and the now forgotten Sir William Beveridge with his plans for looking after us from the cradle to the grave. There was the Big Brotherdom of the Webbs, christened as such by Orwell but now known as the welfare state. The cult of the State presumes that it can solve all our problems, or could do so if the leadership were different. This is still the issue of the next election, and the one after. But the Fabian notion of the managerial class and the value of gradual reforms is now part and parcel of civil service thinking, irrespective of party.

It may be perplexing at first sight that the middle-class is not more grateful to Harold Wilson, as it was coming to be towards Clement Attlee. This is due to the ingrained conservatism of the older, and the necessity for the young and ambitious, in that world where one might as well be out of life as out of fashion, to acquire the brand-image of progressive Toryism. Even the professional class, now the bastion of the Labor Party as once the miners were, and in France the last bearers of the parliamentary socialist banner, has become anxious about its place in society. The petty-minded see that no restraints are possible upon the worker, or upon that part of the younger generation that despises bourgeois values. A "right-wing backlash" is hoped for, as the only way of preserving that economic domination which is regarded as the reward for merit. In reality, merit is the result of economic domination.

Why are people concerned for such domination? Money is power and power is privilege. It is at once a symbol of servitude but also of liberty within the system. Yet it is only a fantasy. It would be a suitably ironic gesture if an expropriatory revolution gave as "compensation" the very paper money worshipped by capitalism. It would be amusing to think of the industrial Romanovs sweating it out in exile sitting on bags of their own currency, valueless now that it was no longer a symbol of power. Merely to question the value of money is to raise a cheap laugh. But if money is the solution to our ills, could not governments print more and make us all rich? Why do they not do so and solve their own problems? An entirely mythic answer, arising out of the neo-theological science of economics, was that the amount of currency that could be issued related to the amount of gold held in the bank.

But as that gold was normally invisible to the outside world, it could easily be removed without anyone being the wiser, and when finance and government discovered the con trick that could be worked (they had only to increase their security precautions-nobody knew if the gold was still there) or simply discarded the gold standard, a new answer had to be found. To be sure, people are kept busy digging up gold in South Africa and transporting it to the United States to bury it again. But the economists no longer worship the image of gold. Now they tell us a different story, that currency is related to productivity, though the people as a whole hold fast to a related legend that the natural wealth of the country and its applied labor all comes out of Waterlow's printing works.

The fables of the economists have come to be the great saga of the British people. A government operating by sheer armed force would not have to trouble what its people think. It could ignore their wants and their opinions. But once one has to reckon with the mob, a different set of answers must be given. The commissar may say, "Have they no bread? This, comrades, is due to saboteurs, enemies of the fatherland. We are building up socialism and everyone must sacrifice."

What can the parliamentarian say? He can only talk in the language of the popular economists, and refer to balance of payments crises and national difficulties. His appeals, if they are to have any effect at all, and they rarely have anyway, must be in homespun language. The national affairs are likened to good housekeeping. We are solemnly warned of the dangers of national bankruptcy. Yet what happens in such an event? We do not pay our creditors? Some states, by using the language of patriotism and socialism, present this as a great achievement: "We have seized foreign assets in our country." It is true other nations do not like this. Britain, France, and Spain united for the first time since the crusades when Mexico did not pay its debts, and invaded the country. But even so, when President Juárez paid up, and Britain and Spain withdrew, Napoleon III went it alone. The debts were only a pretext. If an imperialist state has the power to invade and wants to do so, it usually does so. It is unlikely that a bankruptcy by Britain would lead to a blockade by the Swiss Navy.

Economics is an agreed fiction. After the anti-Czarist pioneer Alexander Herzen fled from Russia, his fortune was declared to be confiscated. The astute Herzen had, however, placed it in government securities, which he discounted with Rothschilds of London. The bankers informed the Kremlin that if the bonds were dishonored they would be re-presented on all the stock exchanges of Europe, and his imperial majesty hammered everywhere as a defaulter. This was considered to demonstrate the enormous financial power of the Rothschilds, who could defy the most despotic autocrat in the world.[15] Both the might of the Rothschilds and the czar were myths of the nineteenth century. Within a man's lifetime, all a czar's commands were insufficient to get him a glass of water. And when a Vienna Rothschild found his wealth confiscated by an even worse despot, the London house did not make themselves the laughingstock of Europe by huffing and puffing at Hitler in the same way.

The Czar had capitulated to Rothschild fearing that an act of legitimate sovereignty would be represented as an act of bankruptcy. As he shared a common illusion, he could be forced to obey. He could not send his soldiers to the banking house to prevent it insulting him—if they had been living in Russia, finance would have yielded to brute force. Though the Nazis still frightened the people with the bogey of international finance, one had only to disbelieve in it for it to lose its power.

Yet Marxists were still convinced that the political power and the armed might wielded by the Nazis were "only a reflex" of the real, economic power, even though recalcitrant capitalists and industrialists might be sharing the same concentration camp as they. Once the fact of brute force was established, the tyrant had only to shake his fist for money to be poured into his lap. His commands were then regarded as strength. When a historian says that a particular war "was paid for by high taxes" he does not really mean that it was paid for by the government printing paper money, distributing it, and then taking it back again. This is the incantation, but not the real magic. What he really means is that, by force or persuasion, the people had to work harder and get less and be subject to greater inconvenience. Sometimes it is done by slavery and subjugation, but this has nowadays a flavor of illegality about it, even though the State legitimizes it. (In defeat, as shown by the Nuremberg Trials, it can be found to be "illegal" after all.) Certainly it is not the way in a democracy. Some other method has to be found.

Yet a democratic politician, except in time of war, has few common ideals by which to appeal for sacrifice. Resorting to the stop-go economy crisis common to both parties has been the modern British form of democratic compulsion. It has become necessary to dramatize the ledger-book. The cross-entries in international banking are now front-page news and a matter for earnest debate. The theme of politics is always the same-that one must work harder and get less. But the reasons given for doing so vary. At one time, under the inspired leadership of Mr. Churchill, we were offered "nothing but blood, toil, tears, and sweat," but that was to win the war. It was apparently won, but we were still asked, by both parties, for sacrifices. This time it was to win the peace. Such as it was, it appears to have been won, at any rate for a longer period than the previous one. But we were still required to pull our weight and give just that extra effort—this time, so that we could get out of our economic difficulties. We have already moved to the stage where this itself has become a joke. We are told now that all this is just the way of the world and it would be impossibly juvenile to question it. For everybody knows from their own experience that if they do not have enough money there are things they cannot afford, and so it is with the nation.

So the saga of the national prosperity goes on whichever government is in office. It is a convenient repository of legends, told in the native language of capitalism, and handily capable of being expressed in different accents of party consciousness. The stuff of its legends comes from the confusion between the tokens of exchange in one country and those of another, for science has failed to produce a coherent economic system under which capitalism could be run more effectively.

Economists have only been able to suggest expanding the viable area, in a Customs Union, in Commonwealth free trade, in the Common Market. Even so, the artificial barriers make importing and exporting more difficult. This is not what causes depressions and slumps, when the goods are there and the labor is there and all that has happened is that the means of exchange have been so monkeyed about with that the system will not work. In such a situation the money system has completely ceased to have any utility.

Gold, in the Middle Ages, proved to be a means of exchange of undoubted utility. In a moneyless society, too, it may still be essential—to the dental profession, for instance. Coin in its time was a handy means of expediting commerce, rather than barter. Even paper currency had a civilizing influence, circumventing the brute force of feudalism with the mercantile devices of promissory notes, drafts and letters of credit. Embryonic capitalism within feudalism had to legalize usury, and to reconcile it with religion, because by it the merchant could finance the wars and lavish expenditure of nobility and government. Though the usurer was hated for his extortions, and the baron admired for his valor, the former was little more than the tax-gatherer for the latter. He could not grow rich on *coin*, which could be seized or garnished, but on *paper*. It seemed like magic to the superstitious, and it still does. Without the device of credit, trade could not continue. The law was no protection; it was merely a means of defending the basic laws of property for the benefit of the powerful, and enabling tribute to be levied upon commerce.

Reforms at that period, anticipatory of social change, consisted of remedying the laws for the benefit of the merchant. The capitalist was able first to prune, and finally to eradicate, the poison ivy of parasite aristocracy. He dictated the laws in favor of commerce. In the wake of drafts and letters of credit came the modern banking system. Coin ultimately became so debased as to be a pocket alternative to paper, small change of no intrinsic value in itself. But paper has become more than a convenient means of exchange; it is the Mammon for which under capitalism we live and die, love and hate. Paper, not gold, is the symbol of power and privilege. Nobody assesses their deposits in the bank in terms of ounces or pounds of gold. For paper, not gold, is the symbol of power and privilege today. (Even in the non-competitive state where paper may not be supreme in terms of money, it reigns supreme in terms of card-membership!)

And paper has long ceased to be a fair means of barter. The very fact that in a competitive society one can speculate upon the fluctuations of the currency proves it to be considered a valuable item in its own right. Interest charges show that there is a cost of money upon money. The supply of gold at least was conditioned by certain natural factors. The Royal Mint can churn out debased coin, while anyone with an offset litho could print off banknotes if it were not subject to certain legal hazards.

In fact, one could quite legally and freely print one's own tender and people will do so if they can get anyone to accept it. Our checks and notes-at-hand could be taken up by others in consideration of our (real or imagined) reliability. Our issue would then become currency. This is what happens with Scottish banknotes, which Scots readily take on trust and assume to be legal tender, and get indignant when English shopkeepers decline them.

The value of legal tender lies in the authority of the state issuing it. Other forms of issue rest upon trust. Money is subject to the fluctuations of authority and may speedily become valueless except to collectors of ephemera. The banks, however, create wealth out of trust. They deal in invisibility. A growing capitalist's potential is assessed, and an overdraft granted by the process of dipping a pen into a red inkwell instead of a black one. A series of paper transactions follows, which may amount to no more than cross-entries in the bank's own ledgers, or at most in the ledgers of the combined clearing house of a handful of banks. Cash as such is unnecessary except by way of small change to pay the grocer, and even that finds its way back to the banks. Unless the government, for reasons of political policy, imposes artificial legal sanctions, the bank can go ahead and create vast industries out of paper and ink.

How does this economic sequence of command-and-obey operate? Why is it that at a nod of the head and a dip of the pen one can get raw materials dug out of the earth, great factories built, vans and ships moving, executives hustling by plane across the world, careworn women smiling again and paying their shopping bills, elegantly dressed women ordering a second Jag, storekeepers rubbing their hands with delight, and representatives going away with large commissions?

And on the other hand, how can a few cross-ledger entries in the wrong colored ink plunge towns and valleys into misery and cause chimneys to stop smoking and the wealth of the world to be left undisturbed? If the bankers are gnomes, in what does their magic consist?

The Catholic peasantry of feudal Europe implicitly believed in the conjurious craft of the Jews, some of whom were the proto-capitalistic usurers, and transactions on paper seemed the work of magicians. Today the superstitious ask us to believe that a little republic, which has avoided participation in war because of its defenselessness, has become our economic dictator—the meek indeed inheriting the earth— and that as a result our lives should be conditioned to the whims of its least worthy citizens, a handful of grasping financiers.

What is the magic elixir that the British nation is asked to believe exists in the fairy vaults nestling under the Swiss Alps? If you believe in fairies, clap your hands, otherwise the fairy will die. So long as the world believes in the Swiss bankers, they will grow prosperous and powerful and develop blood pressure and ulcers through carrying the world upon their shoulders. Cease to believe in them and all the fairy gold in the vaults turns to ashes when you try to cash it.

It was the logic of feudalism that all gave what they had. The poor man gave his labor. The merchant gave his wealth (his capacity to develop markets). The priest (forerunner of the professional class) gave his blessing. The knight gave his valor. It was a convenient theory for all but those who were not consulted in its formulation. It still shadows Tory thinking. Whatever the proposed reform, the classical lament is "Where will the money come from?" The suggestion is that it can only come out of taxation, which is equally unintelligent as to say "print more." It suggests the rich keep the poor, since wealth comes from taxation and presumably the more one pays the more one contributes "to the less fortunate."

Tory prejudices have influenced the economic thinking even of the reformers, many of whom, even the most advanced, feel that the degree of taxation is bound up with the level of reform, and that those who oppose the monetary system and therefore do not advocate taxation as a remedy must by that token be opposed to reform. An alternative absurdity, frequent in the peace movement in the 1930s and not extinct even today, is that if we saved the cost of a bomber, or what have you, we could send five hundred children from the slums on a seaside holiday each year. And yet one immediately wonders what the building of a bomber has to do with sending children on holiday. Certainly the bomber is quite unnecessary, but all that is needed for the holiday are a few coaches, a bit of free beach, food, pop, and a place to stay. What have the wasted efforts of the engineers got to do with it?

Radical thought can contain an element of resentment against unfairness, which is quite understandable. Surely, if the wealthy are not going to be expropriated, it is only fair that they should be taxed! Through this argument parliamentary socialism has made inroads upon the working class, but in doing so it has postponed expropriation to an unreal future. Once it has done that, all it can do is occasionally to punish the rich with mild slaps. The right-wing, non-progressive Conservative is right in saying that much of taxation is merely punishment. In his arrogance he does not see that these lightly administered slaps save him from a worse hiding. Even in the present economy, it does not make much difference to society whether the wealthy are taxed or not. If each class made its demands firmly enough and consistently defended its living standards, they would attain the same level as they get from the State as concessions. Once they are pushed under, the affluence of those above is of little practical concern of theirs.

But, the bewildered reformer cries, if the rich were not taxed they would be buying second yachts while there would be no funds available for artificial teeth under the National Health Service! It may be wondered if they suppose that a yacht builder can make false teeth, or a dental mechanic uses seasoned timber? Liberalism, like parliamentary socialism, ignores the con trick of the money system, sharing Tory thinking on the real value of money. It is assumed that if one views taxation as illusory, it follows that one opposes reforms as such. Yet increase in human misery is something that happens when people are defenseless, and this lack of power is due to delegating it to others and to trust in the monetary system.

All so-called reformism, when not dealing with restrictions upon social life, is bound up with the redistribution of money. If the palpable falsity of our monetary system is not recognized, and a moneyless society is thought of as an illusion, one cannot avoid credence in the mumbo-jumbo of political thinking.

Revolution, to a "reformist," can only be visualized in terms of the ritual outburst of fictional South American republics. Yet every so often a revolutionary thought may strike the mind even of a mandarin. He is given a fascinating glimpse behind the curtain that surrounds the sacred economic mysteries. For instance, the Paris Metro was seen to spend more on the collection of fares than it received in actual revenue. For political reasons, it could not raise fares. Why not abolish fares, and actually save money by doing so? The taxi drivers protested. An indignant councilor exclaimed, "*Mais c'est l'anarchie!*"

The irrelevance of the money system is seen when needs and luxuries are well defined and largely available, yet some get insufficient for their needs, others get more than enough, and a few get an abundance of luxury. How is this method of distribution defined? How are our abilities rewarded? The yardstick, the reward system, is defined in different ways: wages, salaries, rent, profits, interest, earnings, pensions, allowances. However labeled, they define our place in society. We do not exchange what we have to offer by any fair means. Rewards are in proportion, or out of proportion, to the general wealth. One may by artificial means increase or decrease this proportion, but any normal system of taxation leaves the proportion still exactly the same according to the degree of power held.

Rewards are based upon power. The power determining our rewards may be sanctioned by history, defined by law or fought for. Not unnaturally, those with the greatest rewards like to think of their fortunate circumstances as due to ability, virtue, good training, or inherited right. Yet any or all of these may be unrewarded if there is no power behind them. Coronets may not count for much in a vigorous new country, however it may esteem capitalism; and kind hearts are notoriously insufficiently rewarded.

Power can rest upon shortage, force or legislation. But it is power that determines rewards. In a state-dominated, non-competitive society, there is less grabbing because the system is geared otherwise. But the State must still, to preserve its authority and to keep that vital line of command-and-obey going, reintroduce other forms of reward and incentive. Positive disincentives for those who buck the system exist in "the submerged level."

Free cooperation, without the State, is mutual aid. It is regarded as impracticable. So was mercantile capitalism in its early days (if not thought of as magical, which is the same thing, perhaps). For on what does finance capitalism rest but trust? It has managed largely, but not completely, to back that confidence up by heavy penalties and the formulation of commercial law. But trust can break down. Its disappearance meant the pricking of the South Sea Bubble, and the Wall Street crash. When trust even in the State itself broke down in inflation-ridden Germany of the 1920s, the people reverted to barter. In occupied Germany in the late 1940s they invented a currency of their own in the shape of foreign cigarettes and canned goods, a handy form of exchange which, as a last resort, could even be consumed. This, though stigmatized as the black market and labeled as anti-social, was regarded as enterprising. When, after the First World War, the German people had turned to mutual aid, in the occupation of the factories, the full murder force of the State was directed against them. Elementary barter was less obnoxious to the forces of rule, though it proved that even the collapse of government into weakness and disorder does not prevent life going on somehow.

Under monopoly rule, whether state capitalism or state communism, the system ceases to depend on trust and moves into one of dependence. Rewards are determined by Big Brother and power is in relation to the administration rather than to economic pressure. The current establishment witch-hunt against unofficial strikes is a reflection of the fact that the State cannot tolerate the workers determining their own rewards by pressure, beyond a certain point. There are naturally no objections to the legalization of trade unions providing they play the role of official dragoons. There is a place for official trade unionism in the dependent society, and even military-ruled Spain finds the necessity of creating its own version of a labor front.

Under a monopolistic order of economy there is a new order of merit. There is less place, and in the state-communist version no place, for the self-made millionaire who can manipulate shortages and exploit anomalies. Bourgeois tourists to Russia find that normal business transactions are regarded as crimes. Even within capitalism, however, there are fewer opportunities for the self-made man as state capitalism advances. The methods of business enterprise of only a short while back begin to look criminal. Businesses are no longer built up by the smash-and-grab of laissez-faire capitalism. The men of power are chairmen of corporations rather than independent bosses relying upon the profit motive. The first Lord Melchett built up a vast, competitive capitalist empire. The present Lord Melchett is concerned with increasing his enormous salary as chairman of a state board. Lord Beeching moves from one board to another. His salary when directing British Rail had no connection with the fact that it might make a profit or a loss.

The way to rise under state control is limited, though it still exists, even in Russia, where the officially approved artist or the sycophantic poet fills the place elsewhere occupied by pop singers or entertainers. Otherwise, the caste system is not being broken by the sudden acquisition of large fortunes. Those who already have large stakes in the economy become even richer, but the means of personal advancement is now through examinations, not through the old capitalist virtues of individual enterprise.

The planned state is a process by which we shall have our rewards determined for us, and the virtues are obedience and conformity. Money, which derives from the workings of individual enterprise, may lose its magical qualities. The wage system may become a sophisticated version of the food-and-keep of the slave. For though abolition of the monetary and wage system is an essential step to freedom, it does not of itself imply freedom if need is determined by others.

A free society might ration those goods which are in short supply and cannot be available upon the formula of "each according to his needs." It can have nothing to do with superior decisions upon merits, or the goblin fluctuations of currency. For then it would cease to be free.

Party Lines and Politics

POLITICAL PARTIES ARE ASSOCIATIONS aiming at power. Some times parties represent classes, especially when a ruling class is driven to a last-ditch defense and has to close ranks. But other factors also come into play, such as personal quarrels and ambitions, the drive of a new power elite, historical continuity, ideological differences, or a combination of some or all of these factors.

Materialistic considerations often, though not always, dominate over ideological ones, and tend to fashion the latter. The anti-clerical and free-thinking French bourgeoisie, for instance, found its way back to political Catholicism not by reason of any "light on the way to Damascus" or even by conscious decision, but solely because of general alarm at the way in which the working class had picked up its own iconoclastic beliefs. In the same way, the slaves of Haiti had embraced the republican ideas of their French masters, who thereupon reacted much as would the old nobility. There has been quite some alarm here too, of recent years, in the way in which disillusion with government has spread among the younger generation.

Tories and Whigs were originally differentiated by the more progressive views of the latter section of the British aristocracy, who naturally came to expect that popular radicalism would rally behind them, even at the period when Whiggish attachment to liberty had long been consigned to the past (it was they who deported the trade union pioneers to Australia). Whigs and Tories became indistinguishable, and the party broke up. At that juncture it was the particular contribution of Disraeli to politics that he saw it was illogical that in the new, Liberal Party that inherited the Whig mantle, the urban working class should follow, not their old aristocratic "protectors," but the very Liberal industrialists who were directly exploiting them. According to him, the natural new "protectors" of the exploited industrial workers were the reactionary landowners, who might well oppress the rural workers but had a common enemy with the factory proletariat in the manufacturing class. Given such an alliance, it seemed to him there was no reason why the Tories could not give up, their reactionary views, and become reformers at the expense of the Liberal industrialists. Universal suffrage could then favor the Conservatives—and would "dish the Whigs." The policy was described by Carlyle as "shooting Niagara." The sage reacted to it as did Bismarck when Lassalle tried to persuade him of this "natural alliance" too. It is in the nature of conservatism to distrust leaps in the dark, and "a leap in the dark" is exactly how Tories described their leader's programme. Yet it was a successful leap so far as they were concerned. Disraeli associated it with popular support for imperialism. And quick victories and painless patriotism, allied to a regard for working-class votes, meant that the Conservative Party got, and retains to this day, a degree of that vote. The Liberal Party was totally deprived of the only reason for its existence. For as the capitalist prospered under empire-building, he became an integral part of the ruling class. Joseph Chamberlain took the Liberal industrialists into the Conservative camp, but it was part of a general intermarriage of the top classes. After that, the working class could either look to the Conservative and Unionist Party as its "protector," or form its own party. Eventually that came about. The Liberal Party ceased to have relevance except as an association for personal ambitions, historical loyalties and confused ideologies. The Labor Party, however, took on the old role of liberalism, and found the working class a new type of "protector" in the civil service.

There are always reasons, false only to the revolutionary, for supporting one party against another. Victory for Tweedledum means defeat for Tweedledee. In Austria, the social democrats and liberals supported the fascism of Dollfuss against the Nazism of Hitler. Many who had sworn never to vote Labor again because it had agreed to the H-bomb that could have ended the world, supported it after the Tories brought in a Rent Act that exacerbated the housing problem. Reasons for voting are magnified out of proportion, and made into political issues. It still remains true that parties are reflections of power interests, even though it may not always immediately be possible to identify one party with one class interest.

Some people find it understandably difficult to grasp the complexity of so many parties, once they have graduated from the discovery that there are more than two or three main ones. Understanding is not made easy by the hackneyed image of the parties or ideas standing from right or left like a row of ninepins waiting for the ball to hit them. The seating arrangements of the French Chamber of Deputies, on which the terms "Right" and "Left" are based, were no doubt a convenient way of spreading the crowd around that august body, but leave much to be desired in the way of explaining what political differences are all about, so long after the French Revolution.

Just as the British public has been persuaded by the advertising world that everyone is middle-class and should live up to that standard, so the French Deputies, after the Second World War discredited the Right Wing because of its collaboration with Nazism, all wanted to sit on the left, leaving empty benches on the right. Only the resumed confidence of the Right, when the bourgeoisie felt secure from social revolution (thanks to the Communist Party), saved the Fourth Republic the expense of building a differently shaped chamber.

In many countries, "right" and "left" have been used in a senseless fashion, merely to indicate an attitude to Moscow. For Moscow itself, to be more "left" than they was to be suffering, in Lenin's phrase, from "an infantile disorder." Yet the anarchists, for instance, whatever the newspaper reader might think, are not "more extreme" than the communists; they are at quite a different extreme. Half the defeats encountered by the anarchists as an organized entity have been the result of being persuaded that they are part of a natural "left-wing" progression. The Communist Party is not nearer to the Labor Party than it is to the Liberals, nor are the latter necessarily farther away from fascism than the Tories (Lloyd George, for instance).

Once again we have recourse to a diagram. This supposes that there are two social considerations: individualistic and totalitarian. In the way in which we live, the basic determining factor is either the individual or the State. And there are two economic considerations: competitive and collective. The way in which we work is either capitalistic or socialistic. Ideologies relevant to the present time, not just theoretical adventures of which the inventive political mind is prolific but which fail to relate to current issues, can normally be understood in the relation of their social outlook to their economic. In this sense, the diagram is a rough-and-ready guide to political theory, and one can at least say for it that it makes far more sense than the drawing of a line from right to left, which up to now has been accepted as a suitable illustration.

Anarchists are at one extreme of individualism and they are also at an extreme of the labor movement, or of non-competitive ideology. At the other extreme of individualism is the free-enterprise capitalist, whose views have long been advocated in this country by Sir Ernest Benn and the Individualists, and now by Mr. Enoch Powell—whose defense of capitalism has become over-shadowed by his use of race for creating division. In the United States it is thought of as conservatism proper, and has been advocated as the only possible alternative to "socialism." This type of capitalist thinking is at another extreme from fascism, if one thinks of the latter in terms of Hitler's National Socialism. But because it sometimes employs the same type of thuggery in defense of its interests, or favors a similar set of people, or falls back on anti-race attitudes to make a popular appeal, it is sometimes confused with fascism. "Fascism" has in any case become an emotive word since the war and is often used merely to connote personal violence. It is not a coincidence that movements concerned with the preservation of a

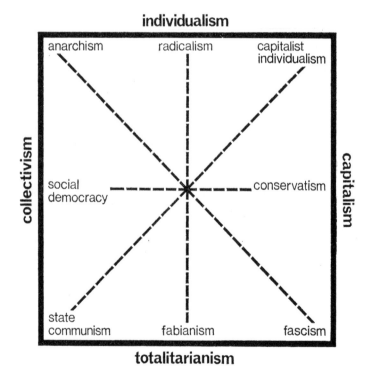

privileged minority or of the State have had to employ violence to keep down the workers. But it has never been individual violence—always organized thuggery of an official or unofficial police variety.

The same confusion has existed between fascism and communism, only because of the degree of violence used by both. The liberal used to say that they were the same thing because they used similar tactics. The term "red fascism" was a good slogan, but false. It was the only term to use, perhaps, if one were to make the straight line intelligible, but it was completely misleading. State communism is a collectivist creed, at the other extreme from anarchism so far as working-class ideology is concerned, though it is also a totalitarian creed, at the other extreme from fascism. When state communism becomes economically "liberated," as is the case in Russia now, it is not moving nearer to the concepts of mutual aid, but towards fascism. It loses its socialistic character and finally becomes, as Hitler's National Socialism would in time have become, a state capitalist amalgam of the two.

In the same way, also, if one dilutes anarchism sufficiently to become "philosophic" or "individualistic" anarchism, it moves in the direction of capitalist individualism. It is already as individualistic as one can go in one direction. To insist upon its individualism to the point of hyphenation is to take it in the other direction. Hence the belief of some American philosophers that it is a "doctrine of the Right," and they confuse the "anarchism" of Thoreau, diluted still more, with revolutionary anarchism. So misleading are the academics that a man can write a book called *Anarchist Thought in India* which is about Gandhi and Vinoba Bhave!

It is equally true that one can dilute anarchism in the opposite direction until it becomes indistinguishable from trade unionism and may ultimately sell out to state socialism; and of course anarcho-syndicalist movements have disappeared from sight because of this trend. The Mexican syndicalist movement is a case in point.

From looking at the diagram one can see what everyone knows to be the case, but which cannot be expressed by a straight line from right to left, that anarchism and fascism are opposites in one sense, and state communism and "Goldwaterism" in another. But at the same time anarchism and state communism are different in another aspect, just as are the ideas of social democracy and political conservatism. Naturally, all ideologies are not at the extremes, though it is a typical Fleet Street contribution to politics, in part arising from "straight-line" thinking, that what is *extreme* must by definition be wrong.

Political opinion can normally be placed somewhere along the sides of the square, if not at the extreme corners. Fabianism, for instance, comes somewhere between state communism and fascism and has (as Bernard Shaw perceived) affinities with both. It is the doctrine of state capitalism. State communism and fascism differ on the fact of class structure within society. Fascism preserved class distinctions, with a bureaucracy. State communism has no classes under the bureaucracy. Fabianism tries to identify the bureaucracy with the ruling class.

If important parties cannot be placed neatly in the square, it is usually because they are coalitions of differing ideas and interests— Democrats and Republicans in the United States, for instance. In Britain, the division between parties seemed more clear-cut at one time. But the Labor Party today is a coalition, too. It is not a working-class party as such, though its rock-bottom votes come as a result of people thinking it is. It cannot be equated with theoretical social-democracy, though some of its protagonists are democratic socialists. It has the duty, often neglected, of defending trade union and cooperative interests, but it has links with management, too. Its middle-class Fabian thinking dominated parliamentary tactics, though again, some of its MPs have been toned-down state communists, their idea of socialism late Lenin or early Stalin, adapted to democratic ideas and rejecting the violence associated with Bolshevism rather than the general theory.

Many more Labor MPs, brilliantly educated and with degrees in sociology and political views fashioned in debate at the Oxford Union, have naturally no conception of socialism at all, and think it has something to do with the nationalization of industry pioneered by Bismarck or the degree of reform passed in a single session. Others are parliamentary liberals who have left the sinking ship. More still have no differences at all with the Conservatives other than the clear necessity of getting a seat, and among these are the hired lawyers used to pleading any cause for which they get paid. There are not a few, graduating from local politics, who hug the fond illusion that the electorate chooses them for their personal qualities and public devotion.[16]

It is difficult to place the Labor Party accurately in Figure 8, as if it were a concrete philosophy rather than a united front. The nearest one can get would be to draw a line from social-democracy to radicalism, and from social democracy to Fabianism, completing the triangle with a line from Fabianism to radicalism. Having done that, one will still find a millionaire MP with laissez-faire views on capitalism outside the neat triangle. When we turn to the Conservative Party, we can draw a triangular corral bordered by economic individualism, fascism and the centre, outside which only the occasional maverick wanders.

There is a certain similarity of idiom along the lines. Philosophies have common ancestry, as do men and monkeys, but the similarities need not deceive us. Often the same cliché is used to signify something utterly different. "The State is our enemy" is often repeated all along the individualist line; devotion to the State along the totalitarian. But some of those who talk of sacrificing for the State see it only in its idealized family role as the nation-state. So they talk with awe of those who "died for the State" when they themselves do not even want to pay their income tax to the State. The term "workers' control" is used not only by those who believe the workers should directly control the industry in which they work, but also by those who advocate more participation in management, the election of officials or even just the fact of saying this is the policy of the State when it is nothing of the sort. ("Spain is a Workers' and Peasants' Republic," said the constitution of the country which appointed General Franco to his command, and much the same sort of thing is said in countries of Eastern Europe today.)

Impassioned pleas for the State not to intervene sound much the same along the individualistic lines, but the nearer one gets to capitalism the more it is "necessary" for the State to intervene in its repressive role, or for that role to be taken over by a private police force. It is natural that the climate in which theories are nurtured will affect them. The individualism that has grown up in the workers' movement is different from capitalist individualism. Totalitarianism differs in the same way. Yet it is a fact of power in the modern world that whoever aspires to rule, irrespective of all these ideologies, must fit themselves into the pervading system of state capitalism. The modern State is too powerful to be fashioned by theory. It must either be abolished or it will shape the party that rules it. Even those aspiring to abolish it could act no different, if by some freak of chance they took power. It is for that reason that revolutionary anarchism opposes party formation and participation in government. Once one finds oneself in office or power, one ceases to be a revolutionary, no matter what one's affiliations might be.[17]

It is implicit in the party programme of today that the impersonal nature of the modern State shapes the parties, rough-hew it as they may. That is why they concentrate on personalities and reformism. Only by a thoroughgoing revolution could a party change the State, but the genuine authoritarian revolutionary is like the Loch Ness Monster—if he were anything more than a legend, he must now be all but extinct. The authoritarian communist mainstream of today is polluted by the effluent of the Comintern, and gives off the stink of patriotism. What is described as "the Left" talks in the language of nationalism.

It is understandable that internal pressures force the Kremlin back to Holy Russian chauvinism, and that in Eastern Europe the politicians have to resort to racial denigration and division to take the heat off themselves. But even in opposition, that part of the "Left" which is influenced by Moscow or Peking, and even by Havana, can only fall back on patriotic gush to explain itself. Those who "support the heroic struggle of the Vietnam people under the great Ho Chi Minh against the Yankee aggressor" might as well have said the same thing about "the heroic struggle" of the British under Churchill, the Russians under Stalin or the Americans under Roosevelt; and in retrospect would still do so. They might not go on to eulogize the struggle against the Hun aggressor under Lloyd George and Clemenceau—not to mention Czar Nicholas—because Lenin made his views known on that conflict at the time. As he has become a god, his opinions are unquestioned by the faithful, but need not be pushed by analogy too far.

If the authoritarian communist has fallen into the trap of talking about national liberation and forgetting about social revolution, the danger for the libertarian is to fall into reformism. Once the near-impossibility of changing the State is accepted, and it is assumed, inaccurately, that it is therefore also impossible to *abolish* it; or, accurately, that this cannot be done without revolution and those with pacifist ideas reject this, one is driven to the position of liberalism. The militancy with which liberal ideals might be advanced does not make them revolutionary. Revolution has to do with social and economic change. Except in the transition to capitalism (in the American Revolution, for instance), even a liberal with a gun is not a revolutionary but an armed liberal. It may be necessary under a dictatorship to fight for so elementary a "reform" as free speech, but if one does not understand exactly what the issues are, one finds oneself fighting for any political leader or nation-state that happens to use "free speech" as a slogan.

In a dictatorship, reformism and revolution might be working on parallel lines. This is the case in Spain today. The Roman Church has for years backed the fascist filly but, always anxious to hedge its bets, now places its money on the Christian Democrat opposition. It even shares a stable with the Communist Party. A "democratic opposition" has been set up, including the "Comisiones Obreras," to make sure that if Franco goes, the alternative will not be social revolution but a liberal, Catholic state without American bases.

Yet it cannot be denied that this opposition is working against Franco and stirred the students. Militant democracy is on parallel lines to this active reformism. But even social-revolutionary movements in Spain are acting in the same direction, since it is towards the overthrow of the present regime. For them to be *deceived* by the democratic opposition would be a disaster, even though they may be working with it.

Party lines may coincide with the class struggle but they have nothing to do with it.

Ideologies originate from common sets of economic or social principles. The use of them for the conquest of power is part of a struggle between rulers and ruled.

Reforms and Revolution

ANTICIPATION OF WHAT IS COMING anyway tends to be regarded as reform. It is possible, at the time of writing, to see a classic monument to liberal do-goodism in Victoria Embankment Gardens, where one of the typically useless London statues to forgotten nonentities is raised. Epitaphs are notoriously inaccurate, but here we are asked to admire "William Edward Forster, 1818–86, to whose wisdom and courage England owes the establishment throughout the land of a national system of elementary education." Could one better it for an outrageous lie? Mr. Forster was no doubt a worthy man, but does England really owe its elementary education to him? When he was born, England was largely illiterate, and when he died it was largely literate, but was he responsible? Without him, would England have remained illiterate, surrounded by literate nations? Could it be that if he had not reminded Parliament of the need for elementary schools, it might have been overlooked altogether? This is what liberals once believed, just as Roman Catholics once believed that St Augustine brought Christianity to these islands, and the patriotically superstitious believe that Winston Churchill won the war.

Individuals are credited with achievements far beyond their power, and we are expected to be grateful. It does not take much intelligence to realize that for some achievements, good or bad, we are entirely responsible ourselves. We are asked to honor Rowland Hill for introducing the penny post (which subsequent reformers have taken away) and even the many prison reformers who have made our jails what they are. They could, of course, be worse.

Not all reforms are useless. The most useful ones may be those that do in fact anticipate coming change. It was impossible, for example, that Britain could have carried on much longer in the modern age hanging people for petty thefts or imprisoning them for life because of debt. The fact that these laws did linger on for so long has left its impress on modern thinking, so that some of what are served up as "reforms" are anti-reforms. Some of those who clamor for the restoration of the death penalty, for instance, regard it as a panacea. One has only to read the letters in the press to see that they are under the delusion that hanging murderers will deter all crimes of violence and even prevent vandalism in the parks.

Other reforms are only recognitions of fact. We owe it to the first post-Second World War Labor government that the Witchcraft Act was abolished, and we can worship whichever devil we choose, provided we do not infringe the Blasphemy Act which it was deemed inexpedient to amend. There are some reforms which are genuine concessions from the State, and are the stuff of politics. But politicians as a class are parasitical upon society, and it is not to be regarded as kind that they give back a few crusts of our own bread, though this is how the press personalizes particular actions of the Chancellor of the Exchequer.

By granting some such concessions to the formerly "submerged tenth," the State has legalized poverty. Work was once the idol. Those who could not get work, and had no way of making others work for them, fell into the pit. The post-First World War reformers, still idealizing work as such, thought one had only to provide work, however unnecessary, for "the unemployed," and that by expenditure on public works they were solving the problem and making money flow again. But it was not the useless toil that solved the problem of the unemployed put on New Deal public works—it was the fact of having spending-power again. The new liberalism accepts the idea of "relief" or "assistance" no longer presented as an act of charity, but as a recognition of the fact that the well-being of the State requires a class at the bottom which is a threat to any complacency or militancy of other classes, yet which does not have to be starved to the point of desperation.

The purpose of social benefits is to encourage flexibility and mobility, or in other words to persuade people to move around as the State wishes, without being physically forced to do so. But its existence also gives the political reformer the chance to take over from the social philanthropist and to play Santa Claus at no expense to himself and in fact as an advertisement for the store.

The competition between political Santa Clauses is so great that few politicians are quite prepared to come out and say that, for their part, they would abolish him. But they are nevertheless concerned that if social benefits are of a certain level, a few people might "abuse" the system. Like the old-fashioned publican they are afraid someone will take the free lunch without buying the beer.

In the jungle of state-controlled society, people do not like to believe that someone, somewhere, without the power to demand it, is getting something for nothing. They fail to see that something is in fact given for something. Those subsidized by the State for whatever reason are considered necessary by the State, even if the stigma of charity still lies upon some institutions. A policeman may be parasitical upon society, but he is not considered to be so as he is essential to the security of the State. Equally so, a prisoner may not be contributing anything to society, but the State regards a standing population of prisoners essential to the enforcement of law. The modem State also regards as essential a growing number who live upon social security, or have low incomes augmented. This phenomenon promises to become part and parcel of future state economy, as it already is in some American cities.

Some sociologists have said that such people are not "exploited" for they are subsidized to live. The public regards them as "parasites" because it has been taught to object to people being idle out of their proper class. Those concerned may not be productive, except by way of children, but they are not the only class that is divorced from production. Social exploitation exists as well as economic, and is sometimes distinguished from it only by semantics. The Victorian gentleman who kept an under-footman at two pounds a year all found was not exploiting his labor in the *same* way as he was that of his workers in a factory, but was the difference of importance?

A modern illustration is that of the Arabs displaced by Israeli conquest and living in refugee camps on United Nations handouts. They are not economically exploited by the "host" countries as were, say, the European immigrants to the U.S. But the latter fared far better. Those politically exploited become essential to the politicians. Wherever institutionalized "charity" exists, the bureaucracy needs the recipients. Without them, it would grind to a halt. They are like the fabled wolf-killer, who had to breed wolves on the sly in order to keep his job. But there is more than just the need to have a children's party so that one can still go on playing Santa Claus.

The State, in order to survive, needs many strata of society which are not productive and some of which are deliberately kept in idleness. The idleness of luxury is the carrot, and the idleness of want is the stick. The fact of modern abundance could make equity possible, but it also makes inequity more workable. Those at the top can literally reach the moon. Those at the bottom need not be starved to the point where they can become dangerous.

The danger is that if the State is allowed to continue on its present course, the technological revolution will squeeze the working class out of production. It may find itself, if not on permanent social security, at any rate performing the menial tasks of the superior classes, regardless of social usefulness, but only to maintain the distinction. Where would be the joys of reaching the top if there were nobody beneath? The truth, despite the admen, is that we cannot *all* be "middle-class."

A working class completely deprived of its productivity, and so of its power (which is there, whether it uses it or not) to change society, might nevertheless become militant. That is one of the signs in the younger generation. One suspects that many advocates of state control hope that it might, without industrial power, become grateful for reforms from the top or permission to participate in some of the decisions made for it. Such a hope overlooks human nature. Nobody is really grateful for what is "done for them." The people living in the Negro ghettos of the U.S. deride such gratitude as "Uncle Tomism." Sooner than be put in a dependent position by the welfare state they would prefer to pull the whole rotten system down—"Burn baby burn!"

While this may sometimes be expressed in misleading slogans, such as "Black Power," the actual fighters are really against power as such and only demand it on the terms they know they will not get. The federal government would welcome a few black militant leaders in power, but the problem is that as soon as they attain office they not merely cease to be militant, which is expected, but they cease to be leaders. They can only lead by running ahead of the crowd: they do not control. What the crowd is saying is "To hell with white liberalism." They are not only against intolerance, but against damned insufferable tolerance too. They are not really revolutionary: "black liberalism" is only liberalism with a gun, and no number of civil rights adds up to social revolution. But as they have no faith even in the reforms for which they are fighting the fiercest, they may achieve a revolutionary position that will shake the world. The tragedy of Martin Luther King's assassination, from the bourgeois point of view, was that here was a moderate and pacific man who was making a bid to capture leadership. The English ruling class might initially have imprisoned him, as they did Jawaharlal Nehru and Jomo Kenyatta, but they would have come to realize that he was useful to them. The more bigoted of them might have gone so far as to object when he was eventually included in the honors list. To have shot him was to show that there was no compromise. If even those preaching conciliation with the dominant are to be killed, what is the deterrent to rebellion?

Even the most intolerant dictator likes to show that there is some hope even for the most recalcitrant. Conquered Spain does not grant remission to its native prisoners, and does not always release them even when their sentence has expired. But every time a prisoner is let out of prison (for they cannot all be kept forever) it is presented as an act of clemency by the *caudillo*. The constitutional monarch has less opportunity for such deeds of mercy.

Mohammed tried to be kindly and tolerant when he decreed that everyone who freed a slave would be certain of a place in Paradise. He did not foresee that his liberal reform would mean that slavery would linger on in Muslim countries long after it had become obsolescent elsewhere; for how else would the ruling class assure its place in Paradise?

We must accept reforms in the spirit in which they are offered, and if, in order to get a political prisoner released after twenty years in jail, we were asked to appear in our shirts like the burghers of Calais and march around a cathedral carrying a penitential candle, this would be an act of solidarity no less than attacking a Spanish bank or kidnapping an ambassador. It is sometimes necessary to eat a peckful of dirt when appearing before a judge. Defiance may no doubt be judged in idealistic terms as to degrees of heroism but has no significance in terms of reality or revolution.

Bakunin, spending years in a Russian jail after the 1848 revolution, indulged in an orgy of self-abasement "confessing his crimes before the Czar" and proclaiming his repentance. These pleas were later published by the Soviet government. Bakunin observed the essential rule: not to inform on or incriminate anyone else. It is difficult to see why his behaviour should be regarded as any different from wearing a disguise to escape, and why his idolizing biographer and bibliographer, Max Nettlau, criticized the releasing of these papers. It is true that the nineteenth century was sold on idealistic postures, and had it been known he "capitulated" it would have damaged Bakunin's reputation for heroism.

What would be the grossest superstition—and this is the analogy with reformism—is to believe that simply by appearing in sackcloth and ashes and traipsing around the cathedral, the dictator could be persuaded to release the prisoners. He might make that his condition of surrender, as an act of humiliation rendered to the conqueror. It is another matter to believe that by carrying out such an act spontaneously, one will have any influence upon him. Letters to members of parliament, discussions of civil rights and the abstract rights of man, petitions to the United Nations, public statements for which one must angle for "names," the collecting of thousands of ordinary signatures . . . all these are secular, democratic versions of the sackcloth and ashes, required by the despot. We may need to engage in them, we may benefit from them, but we do not have to be fooled by them.

This type of liberalism is like learning the captors' language in a prisoner-of-war camp. It makes communication between jailer and victim easier. It may help the jailer to give his commands, but then there is a possibility that otherwise the prisoners might face extinction. The captive is able to have some concessions granted, though at the expense of a promise not to escape (which may be ignored). Once the language is learned, and especially if it is mastered, brainwashing is possible. The only way to resist brainwashing is by non-cooperation, for going along with it spells destruction. The prisoner-of-war is driven back to the art of shirking, which (and not conscientious objection, revered by English pacifists and liberals) is the true art of resistance to the Army—it was not a coincidence that Hašek, who wrote *The Good Soldier Schweik*, the classic of shirking, was an anarchist.

On idealistic grounds one may argue as to whether rejection of parliamentary reformism is "purist" and "sectarian" or not. From a viewpoint immersed in legalism, the acceptance of "mercy" under the law when one regards law as conquest may be regarded as inconsistent and even equated with the attitude of the totalitarian who wants free speech for himself but denies it to others.[18]

The libertarian does not fight against all reforms. But he should be careful to make them identify themselves first. And then give only his name, rank, and number.

Sectarianism and Unity

ONCE A SLOGAN BECOMES POPULAR, it is appropriated for general use though it may be given vastly different meanings. To an outsider from any movement, there must seem to be a proliferation of sects saying or going round much the same thing. This is said of the revolutionary movement of our times. It was equally valid of the French Revolution. Even in the wake of the Reformation came the diverse sectarianism of the Protestant revolutionaries, when some of the approaches to spiritual problems were made which are now applied to social ones. There was, too, a reflection of the class struggle following economic changes.

But the term "sectarianism" is not a reproach. The British revolutionary movement has proceeded from sectarianism. All its achievements have been under sectarian banners. Unity is strength, but expressing opposite points of view within one organization is only cashbox unity, which gives cashbox strength. The saving on overhead expenses has nothing to do with an adventure of the mind or a determination of will.

Economic changes can only come about as a result of unity at the places of work. Workers' councils, united with others, industry by industry, and locality by locality, are the basis of a revolutionary movement and also of a changeover in the system. It is possible now "to build the new society within the framework of the old," by the creation of units in industry; localized associations for mutual aid and protection; cooperative endeavors and even clubs of common interest. A living commune consists of all facets of human interest. A united, local commune can bypass the State and ignore laws imposed upon it that it does not wish to observe, unless the authorities use force. And a commune active in coordinating workers' councils, tenants' associations, and many other action groups would be the fallback unit in any creation of a free society. It circumvents the need for the State and thus negates authority. It makes it possible for the State to be abolished.

It is not supposed that such a movement could be composed entirely of conscious libertarian revolutionaries. This would not be envisaged by the "sectarian" but the very people who would say they are against sectarianism would presume that it should be so. It is accepted that within any workers' council or local commune that might now be created, there would be many political trends and ideas, including authoritarian ones. That in itself does not make the movement less libertarian or less revolutionary. A free society is one in which repressive institutions are abolished. As they are there to ensure economic domination, the end of one means the end of the other.

The fundamental mistake that lost the Russian Revolution was allowing *parties* to be represented within the councils by individual delegates. The soviets did not consist of "delegates of workers, soldiers and peasants," as was at first presumed; but of parties. Orators like Lenin and Trotsky were certainly not workers or soldiers, far less peasants. They became leaders of the councils by virtue of being leaders of their party. Their rise to power was through years of party intrigue. As journalists (if that were their profession) they had a slim chance of representing the printworkers' soviets. As leaders of their party, they were prominent figures—big fish in a small pond.

It would not matter that delegates to committees were, outside the committee, members of political parties or religious bodies. Experience shows that those politically committed will certainly form associations outside industrial or tenants' committees which will give them assistance in their work inside. A strike committee will gladly take help from an outside body. It takes it less gladly when the outside body, using the magic words "ad hoc" and "liaison," wants to take over control.

Still less does it matter when one goes past the stage of having delegated committees, and adopts the principle of the mass-meeting. But since, even so, there will be this type of propaganda with which to contend, the anarchist—accepting that real unity is on the social and economic field—will find it necessary to be able to express libertarian views to counter the authoritarian views. For this he needs his outside support, too. Some form of sectarian organization becomes inevitable.

For those with experience only of authoritarian organization it appears that organization can only be totalitarian or democratic, and that those who disbelieve in government must by that token disbelieve in organization at all. That is not so, but it may be admitted that to the revolutionary anarchist, there is no purpose as such in forming a numerically strong, financially sound or even politically effective amorphous body. Within what is vaguely thought of as the libertarian movement, there may be various trends, though many are invented for the purpose of discussion. Amorphous unity has an attraction for the amorphous journal or the amorphous grouping, which spawns freely. It may grow around the leader without a following, who perhaps has been elected by the press or TV to an eminence he has not yet attained, but may well do so "by unity." It is not through united fronts of such a kind that one can change the economic problems of society.

It has become recognized as a danger within any revolutionary movement that it may emulate the religious sects, in that a "well-known person" may lay down what may well be an excellent programme for revolution, to such an extent that he will be worshipped years after his death. The relic of his followers will group themselves in small parties in his remembrance, and be absolved from any necessity to follow the programme. Or the revolutionary himself, because of his own programme, postpones any revolutionary action that falls short; in such an event, it is just as much a means of adapting oneself to the system as the belief in reforms or the adaptation to careerism. Or, economic action being thought of as the only form of direct action, the revolutionary enters the trade union movement and is immersed. Alternatively, he sees there are other forms of direct action but cuts himself off completely from industry.

The task of the revolutionary is resistance to oppression, even if the resistance is that of one person alone. It is not the idealisation of aims. It is absurd to speak of anarchism as a doctrine of love, non-violence, even of freedom. This is a description of society at which we are aiming, but we cannot profess a monopoly in such ideas. We can only say that an authoritarian society makes them impossible and even sound undesirable to those brainwashed by the State. The assertion of these ideas as high ideals but devoid of practicality for lack of economic change in society, or used as a criterion by which to reform present institutions, we have here described as militant liberalism (as opposed to parliamentary liberalism). Thought of as philosophic anarchism, it can become trendy. But the alternative is not ossification. In the International Anarchist Conference at Carrara (1968) the possibility of a traditionalized ossified revolutionary movement became clear.

The press tried to explain the division there in terms of "youth" versus "age," and this is an imposed prejudice of the mass media which could have confused the issue. Ideas held too long without action become ideals. Ideals may inspire. But they can also be kept too long in the fridge.

Revolutionary socialist ideals, without the action that goes with them, degenerate to an endless sales campaign for literature or a perpetual education class (in which "the workers" are "educated to the level of the party consciousness" and it is not even noticed that the standard of the latter has become lower than that of the former).[19] Parties become monuments to dead leaders. However militant the early promise of programmes, the rump that remains when these have been postponed—simply because it has not degenerated into reformism—cannot of its nature be militant. The profession of anarchist ideals is no guarantee against this. Ossified revolutionary movements, though they may object to the description of "party," become dead political parties. Syndicalist movements may become large, and therefore be compelled, in order to serve their members, to bargain with capitalism. Anarchist movements may fall into bureaucracy in an endeavor to preserve property against outside takeover. An ossified federation is only a memorial to past activity, and this proved at Carrara to be the case with many of those represented, in particular those preserving, in exile, a past historic role.

It seems (at any rate, to the writers of this book) that the alternative is sectarianism. Even a movement based upon activity can become ossified in the future. Unity with other organizations is to dilute revolution, not to foster it. The holding of ideals in the abstract is an interesting philosophical exercise. Applying them to current social problems is a chimera. To make an organization active or even effective is of little ultimate use, since it tends to compromise, ossify or vanish. The struggle that counts is that which helps to build up a new society, and this can only be aided by the revolutionary individual or group which persistently puts forward its propaganda by word and deed. By our sectarianism we may at present be divided from the rest of the world. But otherwise we are part of the world. We do not accept the absurd contention of Trotskyism that it is necessary to join the Labor Party in order to "be in" among the working class.

The libertarian revolutionary cannot have anything to do with party political organization.[20] It can only be a vantage place for power, or a memorial to past battles, or a spiritual ghetto. It is subject to the pitfalls of bureaucracy or those of takeover. Democratic control is no safeguard, for though majority decision is accepted as an expedient way of doing business, in practice the intake is controlled so that the majority will be in accordance with the decisions to be taken.[21]

What pass off as revolutionary issues, therefore, have seldom any relevance to revolutionary ideas. In degenerated Protestantism, churches and chapels are founded which become new sects, and arise sometimes merely out of quarrels as to whose hand should be in the cashbox, or personal differences upon the manner in which business should be conducted, quite as much as over doctrinal disputes. The pattern can repeat itself politically. But it has nothing whatever to do with building a new society.

A Clash of Generations?

THE FACT THAT OSTENSIBLY revolutionary associations can become merely, as it were, the "ex-servicemen's legions" of past struggles may mean that there will be older people in ossified movements, and younger ones in currently active movements. On the other hand, in some of the rebellions of today, though composed almost entirely of students, past philosophies such as Blanquism, Trotskyism, De Leonism, stride around with a fixed gaze like the undead. The idea of classification by "generation" really comes from the university curriculum.

In the world in general, however, one finds that "the generation clash" is another abstract conception used to enslave. It is like the metaphysical idea of "the majority." Everybody knows that "the majority" do not support revolution. If they did so, there would be one. To "consider public opinion" and "respect majority decisions" is to place oneself entirely in the hands of politicians who maneuver such opinion and decisions. The *idea* of the majority is in itself a means of persuasion to adopt the opinions attributed to the majority.

Once one goes against those opinions, one will be regarded as a "minority." The conception of a generation gap transforms what is becoming a majority, into yet another minority whose opinions "we" naturally respect or treat with the contempt they deserve, according to "our" degree of liberality. For the art of rule by persuasion is to redefine according to necessity the distinction between "us" and "them."

Driven to admit that there is, perhaps, some tension in society, when perhaps overwhelming pressure brings industry to a standstill or barricades to the streets years after the liberals had dismissed the notion as "dated romanticism," the journalist invents the theory that this constitutes a clash of generations. Youth, after all, is not a permanent condition, and a clash of generations is not so fundamentally dangerous to the art of government as would be a clash between rulers and ruled.

The explanations of the mass media are not only accepted by the bourgeoisie and framed into social theories by the academics, they become accepted gladly by pseudo-revolutionaries and mistakenly by real ones. Some French students who have rejected the class war, think there is an age war. "The young make love, the old make obscene gestures," says one. Does he mean that his virility will cease at thirty, forty, fifty? Do those "new rebels" who state that youth (and imply "educated youth") is the "revolutionary class" mean that they themselves will cease to be revolutionaries when they have graduated? Unfortunately, this is often exactly what they do mean. The ruling class has never objected to Prince Hal spending his days roistering if as King he made good use of them.

It is natural to a property-owning system that there should be a clash of generations in the possessing class, because of the hereditary principle. The eldest son has to wait for the old man to die before he can come into his "rightful" inheritance, and gets a bit impatient. Feudal society was full of this inevitable filial antagonism, well illustrated in the hatred of fathers and sons in the Hanoverian dynasty. This type of generation gap lasted for a long time within the aristocracy, since the eldest son was not willing to go "into trade" (laziness had been idealized) and one of the few ways of easing the pressure was to put him into the Commons before he went into the Lords. It was called "warming-pan politics," and though made difficult by the Reform Bill, has not entirely disappeared.

Economic antagonism between the generations was less prevalent in the bourgeoisie, where the father could take his sons into business, and-certainly in the period when wisdom and respectability were reckoned in terms of the years one had lived-the patriarch sheltered his sons until they achieved business maturity. It is no coincidence that prosperous capitalism was patriarchal. Only the scapegrace son, a stock figure in the era's fiction, waited impatiently for the old fool to die so that he could squander his "good" money away.

The clash of generations was almost unknown in the working class, where the property to be left was negligible or nothing, and all that the virtuous children got out of the old man dying was the expense of the proper send-off. Both father and mother could pass on their skills to their children, and one of the bitterest complaints against laissez-faire individualist capitalism was the way in which the home life of the workers was broken up. The woman, taken from her loom to become an automaton in a factory, could not pass on her home skills to the younger generation, and, as she felt, her children were robbed no less than herself. The workers turned to the British revolutionary movement, the Luddites.[22] So feared was it by the capitalist class that to this day the term has connotations of terror to the bourgeoisie greater than that of "Bolshevik," and enjoys the privilege, with the word "anarchist," of being used as a pejorative word to excite prejudice against something quite different from what it plainly means.

At a time when the older proletarian had been able to amass little or nothing, he was less dogmatically opposed to revolution because of *age*. Once possessed of radicalism, it did not vanish with advancing years. Reformism gave the older worker a stake but also made him captive to it. He needed quick reforms "within my lifetime." Reaction made a division between generations—younger labor came cheaper. The ruling class divides as it conquers.

In more recent times there has been the notion of youth itself as an idealized political concept. It gave the opportunity for new adventure and new adventurists. Democratic feudalism was advocated by Disraeli's Young England, and the end of feudalism by Young Germany. The Young Turks swept away despotism and the Italians brought it back, singing as they did so the official fascist anthem that youth was the springtime of beauty.

One leaves this type of enthusiasm for the attention of the psychologists and sociologists, already as busy as vultures on defeated causes, and turns almost with relief to the careful attitude of the social-democrats weighing up the utilitarian values of young vigor but unwilling to let it take over. In the Labor Party it has always been accepted that there should be a youth section, carefully corralled off, and it has played an important part in building up the party organization. It has been recognized that it is permissible, under a certain age, to become a rebel, and that this may even be a necessary preliminary to becoming a member of the right wing. But whenever the youth organization has been able to express its views, it has inevitably been more dynamic than the parent body, more or less progressive according to the prevailing standpoint, and has equally inevitably been dissolved, or has quit.

The Communist Party, which at one time created this embarrassment for the Labor bureaucrats, now finds itself in exactly the same dilemma with the Young Communist League.

The rebellion of bourgeois youth today against the pettiness and conformity of the elderly bourgeois is not merely a rebellion against age. Those of the former who think it is prepare the way for their later defection when they, too, are elderly and still bourgeois. It is a rebellion against bourgeois values as such, and a conscious choosing of values other than those of conquest and rule, or of buying cheap in one market and selling dear in another. By insisting that the present rebellion all over the world is a generation clash and confined to students at that, the makers of public opinion hope that by so defining it they have determined its character.

This is part of the art of rule-by-persuasion. It is no longer generally believed that using this art is a conscious conspiracy by the ruling class. Yet the fact remains that the art exists, even if the idea of "conscious creation" of domination and the attitudes that perpetuate it was no more than an inspiring myth. It may be that by a process of mutation only those ruling classes survive who happen to use these methods.

If this is the case, it is easier to understand some superficial contradictions in the art of government. It would be over-Machiavellian to assume that somewhere a supreme council has decreed that pop groups should make their fortunes supposedly catering to, but in fact trying subtly to influence towards establishmentarianism, the young rebels of today; or why educational grants should be lavishly spent on university research enabling academics to explain to the revolutionaries what they are really thinking; or why politicians need to exploit divisions and antagonisms within society. But it is because they feel that such "spontaneous" movements help the ruling class to survive that many rebels turn to mass demonstrations, feeling that the more they frighten the bourgeoisie, the better, and let them bring out their heavy artillery if they will. For the storm troopers are there in reserve all right, even if some of the gruppenfuehrers are saying not "Sieg Heil!" but "I was quite sympathetic to them until . . . ."

Violence and Terrorism

WE ALL DEPLORE EACH other's violence. Most people, whether they admit it or not, are conditioned by the mass media, the neo-Church, and they deplore the type of violence that the State deplores and applaud the violence that the State practices. Dear old ladies, incapable of upsetting the feelings of a cat sitting on the chair they wish to occupy, passionately demand flogging, hanging, and disembowelment, sometimes even for demonstrators. Lynch law is not "anarchy"; it is that degree of law beyond the State, to which authoritarian thinking can lead. The State itself can invoke vigilantes or fascist thugs. It can give carte blanche to the police when its authority is bypassed or flouted, or where it appears that the State apparatus is insufficient. When it does not do so, lynch-law arises. Yet the same people, from the indignant old ladies to the lynchers and the fascists, will be morally outraged by assassination, since the mass media have not prepared them for this.

After the First World War, the press had barely ceased the campaign against reinstating conscientious objectors in their jobs, when they were deploring the "violence" of the workers occupying the factories in Italy. They welcomed Mussolini's mass violence, and deplored as "violence" the attempts to shoot him. To the pacifist conscientious objector, the criterion being "violence" and not freedom the men who tried to shoot Mussolini were "on a par" with the fascists—"They were using the same methods." Yet common sense showed that those who were nearer to Mussolini were not those who were trying to shoot him, but those who, because they deplored violence, sought to make the population tranquil, and would sooner cooperate than resist; who, although they were not fascists, felt that anything was better than revolutionary "violence." Yet that would have been individual. Fascist violence was mass.

We find there *is*, despite the cynicism of the pacifist, a distinction between *our* violence and theirs. We admire the rebel who tried to assassinate Mussolini, or those who did, in face of an angry crowd, kill the king of Italy, the president of France, the Czar of Russia. It is possible to understand the action of one man against a tyrant. We find it impossible to see a parallel with the violence used by the State: the murders in the concentration camps, the slow deaths in Siberia, the judicial killings, the use of fascist squads to remove political opponents, the firing squad, the mass bombings, the use of methods of wholesale slaughter.

A retired military man, who may have sent thousands to their deaths, will be morally outraged at so nonviolent an exercise as the occupation of homes by squatters, and will write to the press condemning it as "violence." *His* violence was legitimate, so he does not regard it as being violent. A street demonstration obstructing his car would not be legitimate. He inveighs at the *violence*. What really disturbs him is the *legitimacy*. Legitimate violence is a State monopoly, for the State makes the laws. It is not possible for the revolutionary to shift people from deliberately induced apathy, within a framework acceptable to the Metropolitan Police or the capitalist press. Nor is there any way of rebelling discreetly, of challenging public opinion though refraining from offending people's conception of good taste. Nor can one change the economic basis of society to approving nods from the judiciary.

No such means existed in Nazi Germany. It is not possible in Russia today. It is unknown here. Polite persuasion is permitted in this country, but only on terms that render it ineffective. The public can be tickled with feathers, when what it needs, in Heine's phrase, is a violent shove in the ribs with a lamppost. Traditional nonviolent protests, such as Aldermaston, become institutionalized. Their protagonists in due course enter government. The test of demonstrations is not, however, whether or not they are nonviolent. That is a criterion introduced by Christian socialist tradition and inherited by the "New Left." It is not a revolutionary test, which is whether or not such demonstrations disturb the chain of obedience by which orders are transmitted and obeyed.

The use of force is inconsistent with freedom and the more a regime employs violence, the more repressive it is. Resistance to force, however, is the first essential to achieve freedom, even if one has to employ violence to do so. The violence that is practiced by the State is the antithesis of freedom, because it is the means by which rule is maintained. If one can only resist the imposition of the State's commands by violence, then such violence must be a prerequisite of freedom, however illegitimate it may be dubbed.

No crime committed in the history of the human race could match the crimes of governments. To such an extent are people terrorized by capitalism and the State that they are prepared to believe the laws imposed upon them are necessary for their existence. When it becomes plain that these laws threaten society, it is pretended that something illegal is involved. Faced, for instance, with the annihilation of the German Jews, the constitutionalist cannot bear to admit that the whole operation, from Hitler's parliamentary tactics in achieving power, to the laws passed by the Reichstag and dutifully administered by the judiciary, were at the time perfectly legal and constitutional.

If a fascist or a state communist regime achieved parliamentary power here, or if its violent takeover were subsequently legitimized, the same police force as exists now would operate. Its officers would not sacrifice a night's sleep, let alone a pension, at *our* fate—yet the mass media asks us to be sorry for PC Jones if he is jostled by demonstrators.

But the moral code invented by the neo-Church is no more binding upon the revolutionary than the religious code invented by the old Church was binding upon the bourgeoisie once they rejected its authority. "Public opinion," the marketable commodity created by power, would be shocked at any individual act of a revolutionary. However despotic a tyrant might be (and even if he were a rival one) there would be tears for his weeping wife and bereaved children, and a homily on the futility of violence. Nothing would be said of his victims. It is in the nature of the State that the tyrant's victims should be numerous, and the tyrannicide's particular. For the power maniac cannot care who or what stands in his way. Scruples are a handicap to him, though if he can turn other people's scruples to his advantage, he will certainly do so.

If, perhaps, in striking a blow against the vilest autocrat, such as happened in throwing a bomb at the king of Spain on his wedding day, a flunkey were accidentally injured, the press would be "outraged" though the same press failed to understand the lack of patriotism shown by those Spaniards who objected to wholesale slaughter in the Moroccan war. In 1910, during an "outrage" at Tottenham, a boy was shot dead, either by the perpetrators or the police, certainly by accident. Nothing could match the horror of the press until four years later, when the Germans shot a lot more, by design rather than by accident. The British, of course, did the same thing, but this was "accidental" and it was hard luck upon the civilians; an excuse the Tottenham gunmen could hardly have given. Horror at violence in this type of context is pure cant. It is objection to persons doing individually what the State legitimizes wholesale.

The peacetime profession of nonviolence held by all respectable citizens should not be confused with the idealized nonviolence held by the peace movement. Even here, this doctrine contains some element of hypocrisy, for thinking of specific leaders of the declared pacifist movement and even excluding the Quakers who give non-combatant service in time of imperialist war, one finds most of them oppose all war until they find a cause they can support by war. But they will never accept class struggle. Gandhist pacifism, on the other hand, may be revolutionary but is completely authoritarian. Those who look on violence as the worst crime of the State—because they judge everything on its degree of violence—may be right, but it does not follow at all that if the State could rule without violence—if the ruling class could conquer without force of arms—this would be the same thing as freedom. ·

On the contrary, a samurai class which could impose its will by moral authority and gentle persuasion would not be less authoritarian than one which needed to use the sword and the whip. It might be less intolerable to live under. But there is no difference, in the compulsion they use, between a Gandhi and a Mao Tse-tung. Gandhi, by his moral persuasion, might have been the more effective dictator.

The mother who says to her children "I will not punish you, but you have broken my heart" is no less matriarchal than the one who smacks them in temper and forgets it. Though on balance one prefers the yogi to the commissar, it is only while one is not brainwashed by the yogi that he is harmless. Those who, by moral persuasion and superior virtue, can induce the virtues exemplified by nonviolence are not giving us freedom. They are fakir-nazis.

Neither the party nor the ashram should be in a position to take over government in an overthrow of capitalist society. If they should do so, it should be a hazardous enterprise in the face of a rebellious people. Dictators should always have to reckon with the fact that assassination is their professional hazard. All forms of government should have to reckon on the fact of a class struggle. Unless it is an unmitigated tyranny or is representative of a class terrified by a traumatic experience of revolution, it seldom wishes to do so. When a government admits the existence of the class struggle, the police state is said to exist. Social conquest, no longer disguised, is carried out by the police (or, if there is no tradition of public service, by the armed forces acting in a police capacity).

When a state no longer needs to admit this brutal fact of existence, it does not cease to employ police: it sets out, however, to make itself more loved by means of persuasion at its disposal and by giving the police some useful tasks with which to occupy themselves. The police become concerned with traffic control, for instance, which however more socially useful it might be, would hardly be handed to a Gestapo with its hands full. It is like using the army for flood relief.

When the State rests upon national conquest as well as social conquest (occupied France, British India), or when the social conquest is of recent origin and military force (Franco's Spain), the police state is essential. Once the fact of social conquest is generally accepted, the State seeks to persuade the community that it is part of a natural order and even that it is of divine origin.

When the Church was the custodian of moral values, its function was to persuade society of the legitimacy and divinity of sovereign rulers.[23] The neo-Church, via the mass media and new science of sociology and psychology, has taken this task over. It proves to us that rebellion is illegal and even unfashionable, or that revolutionaries hate their fathers (as against the happy family life of the conformists) and will even, given their head, prove that criminals are a racial type or that racial types are criminals. Deviation from State dogmas may be shown as degeneracy. Given sufficient funds, they will teach us all how we may fit into a sick society.

An American psychologist has studied the motives of those who tried to kill presidents of the United States. This type of study is becoming a new national sport. He has come up with the conclusion that it is "a wish for immortality." No doubt—but what lies behind the desire to become president? Many would-be assassins viewed their act "as a stroke of national policy or patriotic heroism." How did the *presidents* view *their* acts? It completely escaped the vision of the psychiatrist that the greater the tyrant, the greater the need for assassination. Those rebels who tried to kill European dictators may have been less delinquent than the pilots who bombed Germany and Italy. The latter may have viewed their murders as national policy and patriotic heroism—there was a great deal of encouragement to do so at the time.

But it is, of course, completely beyond the province of the psychiatrist to inquire into the causes of war. The sociologist has no such qualms and he will even endow the impersonal State with human qualities in the way that the early Church invoked its divinity. A "country" is looked on as a real person, with anthropomorphic attributes. Children growing up after the First World War found it hard to understand that Belgians were really not necessarily "poor" nor "little"; and after the Second World War it was difficult for them to understand that Poland was not, in fact, a "small" country. Still less was it possible to understand that all Americans were not rich and powerful. More importantly, the term "aggression" applied to a national act has completely misled everyone. Many reformers sincerely believe that "aggressiveness" causes wars. It is one of the reasons that the sport of boxing gets so many critics (especially those who, like Baroness Summerskill, began as pacifists and ended, though politically committed to the atom bomb, still opposed to "aggressiveness"). Yet the professional boxer is lucky to become a P.T. corporal in time of war—he is more likely to be in the glasshouse for his aggressiveness. It is not the Rocky Marcianos who are the good soldiers. The meek, professional diplomat with the bowler hat and umbrella, who begs one's pardon if he is bumped into on the staircase, will embroil the nation in war, and the civil servant Eichmann is the prototype of how he will then behave.

The mere "aggressiveness" of a Napoleon or a Hitler could not cause a war. One can find their like at any street corner. What causes war is the meekness of the many. Obedience enables leaders to pursue an aggressive course.

It was not "the German character" nor even the Nazi ideology that caused the German army in the last war to behave in a way that provoked resistance. It was conquest itself, made more obvious by the fact that the conqueror was foreign, and more painful by the fact of its being Nazi. The diplomats tried to hide the plain fact of conquest by creating "legitimate governments" that paraded the shabby old patriotic colors. In occupied Russia the Germans had the chance of being regarded as liberators, but Nazi ideology regarded the conqueror as a superior class and acted accordingly. It was painfully obvious in the Ukraine that the Soviet ruling class had been replaced by an invading ruling class that regarded the Ukrainians, as natural helots. Nazi ideology prevented Germany from disguising the naked fact of a police state in arms.

Resistance throughout Europe was given a national-patriotic ideology largely by the London-based propagandists whose active part in the struggle consisted of encouraging radio speeches and intrigues with British diplomacy. So far as those on the spot were concerned, resistance to the police state was unavoidable. The Communist Party, talking in the language of the *class struggle* but in practice obeying the *political necessities of the Russian government*, was able to persuade the underground movements that these two opposing matters were identical.

The Communist Party of today does not entirely deny that there is a class struggle, but it does its best to adapt its terms to those of national patriotism, since it serves the interests of the Kremlin. The liberal, and usually even the pacifist, would deny there is a class struggle at all, which we find a strange attitude. Much as we oppose national war, we would hardly pretend it did not exist. It is hard to define a nation, and imperialism has made the lines blurred. Nor are racial differences confined to opposing nation-states. It is highly desirable that such wars should not exist. Yet they do, notwithstanding our disapproval. It is more difficult to define a class war because there is a degree of voluntarism.

The nation-state can say, in regard to national war, what the law is; who are its subjects and whom for the time being it considers not to be its subjects. Even to press a national claim based on race, as against power, is to commit treason (as Sir Roger Casement discovered). Unless the State chooses, even ideological affinity is not recognized but as treason. (Joyce and Amery were hanged, though several hundred Germans, in British employ, had committed exactly the same "offence" as they.) Successful treason is impossible, since it then becomes the highest patriotism. Many of the "Old Bolsheviks" were executed for "collaborating with fascism" a few years too soon. All this is part and parcel of the terrorism of the State.

The state cannot, however, normally admit the fact of a class war, because this would be to sanction counter-terrorism by the people. Once it is obliged, by the creation of a police state, to admit the fact of a class war, the response is always the same. It can be seen in Czarist Russia when the Police State was opposed by individual acts of violence, which were the only means of protest. Acts of "terror" against the Spanish police state have announced to the world that there can be no compromise with the Franco regime.

The manner of these acts causes an alliance between the "constitutional and democratic" police forces, and those police forces which are acknowledged to be no more than an armed conspiracy against the people. There was an entente between the Western police and those of Czarist Russia, when the Kremlin established a political police bureau combining diplomatic intrigue, espionage and anti-revolutionary activity, which, with its lavish bribes and employment of agents-provocateurs, corrupted everything it touched.

Public concern prevented the Nazi cooperation with the democratic police forces being too well publicised, though it is exemplified by the head of the French police, M. Chiappe, handing over the dossiers of the revolutionaries to the Gestapo in 1940. The British police then, and since, declined to give an assurance that they would not do the same thing in the same circumstances.

When the bourgeoisie becomes "terrorized" it is "provoked" into using the police and shows the true image of social conquest. In the United States the bureaucracy is so efficient in the silent art of mass destruction that the young rebels have spat upon bourgeois culture and taken the responsible attitude of "irresponsibility"—both from revolutionary hope and from new despair they "provoke" the police so that persuasion has to stop and is replaced by force.

Even back in the legendary days of Robin Hood, violence was justified once social conquest was recognized. It not only justifies the revolutionary, but also, at any rate to himself, the criminal. What is wealth but the accumulated thefts of the past? How did the titles and the ownership of land arise? Once it is appreciated that the accumulation of property is due to theft, but that the robbery goes back in time, it is hard for anyone to understand the argument of capitalist economics that robbery has got to cease now. Why? Because the law says so. The tinhorn gambler wants to quit the game because he is winning. The moral sanctions against disobedience of the State need a lot of honeyed words from the neo-Church to make them convincing.

The present values now described as "bourgeois" are those established in Victorian times, and are a justification of power remaining where it is. The same ethics and morals exist in Russia, though in the economic sense there is no bourgeoisie, for they are those of the power-holding minority. An exaggerated feeling of destiny, chauvinism, sexual Puritanism, and the other feelings arising from power on the one hand and abnegation to the State on the other, are characteristic of rising capitalism and of Soviet Russia. In both cases a stable ruling minority is in triumph over a successful State that acts as a façade to human misery. In both cases some form of mass terror became necessary. In Victorian England it was poverty, in Soviet Russia political repression. In both cases, the only antidote, individual terror, became apparently anachronistic because of the success of the media of persuasion. In one, such action seemed unnecessary because of the "continuous advance of suffrage" and in the other because it has been identified with "capitalist and fascist sabotage of socialism." Resistance in both cases became sullen, nonviolent, resigned.

In all political history there is a feeling that "Things may be bad, but let them not get worse." It increases as one gets older, and breeds on defeat. It is the case against militant action, and against holding individual autocrats responsible of acts of tyranny "for fear of the backlash."

Fortunately, there is renewed hope with every generation. Disastrously for humanity, the State is winning the race—its powers of destruction grow faster than the forces of rebellion against it.

The State, as institutionalized conquest, leads to destruction. Apart from the philosophical discussion of ends and means, it is common sense that one's actions should be conditioned according to one's aims. Our aims are not the conquest of power but the accountability of individuals for their actions. The enemies of freedom should not escape their responsibility by pleading the fact that they acted under orders. At the point where they are held personally liable for their deeds of violence, they fall back on the plea that violence (by anyone else) is "futile."

Pacifism ceases to be ranked with bolshevism and anarchy, and until the State chooses otherwise, the public is completely sold on the futility of "violence," though most of the "violence" against which it inveighs is in protest against mass murder. It is genuinely hard for the average person to understand, in the face of mass conditioning, that a person might be vehemently opposed to mass murder and for that very reason all the more inclined to make a violent protest. One of the present authors, facing a Spanish court-martial as the result of his belief in the removal of dictators, found that some of his friends and relatives genuinely protested his innocence, citing his known opposition to nuclear armament. "He is a pacifist, not a terrorist," they said, and it was inexpedient, whilst on a capital charge, to undertake the obvious explanation. One or two afterwards felt they had been misled. The other of the present writers, facing a British court-martial, was rebuked for his "inconsistency" in opposing mass murder when it was notorious he supported individual violence ("and you cannot deny this from your actions"). It appeared clear to them that if one did not support State violence, or objected to sacrifice for the ruling class, one could not sustain any form of violence and probably not eat meat either. Those who think this is an exaggeration need only refer to some of the imbecilic comments made at conscientious objectors' tribunals.

But violence is not the yardstick. It is not even relevant to social revolution, which has to do with the economic change-over of the system. Violence is only needed to answer terror from above by the imposition of personal responsibility from below. Historically, one sees most ruling classes will fight on to the end rather than give up power, and at that point another ruling minority wants to take over. This cannot be answered by mass terror, for generally the army of those having or seeking power will be superior to any army of those opposing power. It cannot be defeated by non-resistance, for this is exactly what it wants. It cannot be opposed by nonviolent resistance, for this presupposes a trained class of leaders whose rule will be only qualitatively different. Finally imposed power by force can only be answered by individual violence. No dictator is so powerful as to be invulnerable to anyone with an elementary knowledge of chemistry. Those dictators who understand this (like Portugal's Salazar) become invisible rulers, and their modesty and lack of flamboyancy is idealized. They stay in power, and their longevity becomes another virtue until they commit the indiscretion of dying.

Politics is bedeviled by the myth of the "strong man." Just as the State is given the qualities of a person, the person is given the qualities of the State. Little Hitler, who never raised his hand for a blow in anger during his life, was one "strong man." Churchill, doddering in the care of valets, was another. Unfortunate, paralyzed, neurotic Roosevelt; crafty, priest-trained Stalin—these were the great men of the Second World War. They were admired for their "strength," meaning that none of them were averse to setting into motion the techniques of mass murder. Neville Chamberlain's bourgeois scruples at doing so made him "weak." The public at the time were brainwashed by this type of presentation into believing that Hitler was in fact, the physically stronger of the two. One blow with the famous gamp and Adolf would have collapsed. But that is not how politics are conducted. Those who, in 1939, believed the official story that war was due "to one man only" did not see the simple alternative to war.[25] They accepted that the only alternative was submission.

Why do the mass media become hysterical at the idea of manhandling statesmen? Is it because this destroys the image? Hero figures must, however, be reduced to size. "The great are only great because we are on our knees."

Is a Free Society Possible?

MUTUAL AID IS THE OVER-RIDING principle in human existence. It is greater than that of class struggle, which is the result of impositions upon society. Faced with a child drowning, only those inculcated with the artificial pressures of capitalism will ask what profit he will gain by diving in. Only those coarsened by racially divisive propaganda will ask first about the ethnic origins of the child. Only those who have succumbed to State conditioning will walk around plaintively asking, "What are *they* doing about it? Where are the police, the fire brigade, the coastguards? What do we pay our taxes for?"

Ordinary people practice mutual aid as a matter of course (the lifeboatmen, for instance), or at any rate recognize that deviations from it are a matter of shame. This is not the case with the conqueror. The Scottish crofters and the Irish peasants were evicted by fire. The Nazi bureaucracy had their murder statistics neatly typed and filled. Shipowners let their men go to their deaths in leaking ships, until restrained by law from doing so. The clergy prayed for the souls of the burning heretics.

A society based upon mutual aid is natural to man. The society in which it is not practiced is the unnatural one. Repressive institutions are imposed upon us. They need to be explained away. The free society should need no apologists. Those who query its practicability are saying that certain repressive institutions are essential. Most, however, would agree we could do without *some* of the organs of repression, though there may be disagreement about which of them are dispensable. The many repressive arms of the State include:

The apparatus of government: The legislature; the judicature; the monarchy; the civil service; the armed forces; the police; the party (in totalitarian countries) or the party political set-up elsewhere.

The apparatus of persuasion: The Church (where it is part of the establishment) although in a non-secular State it might be part of the apparatus of government; the press and other methods of information; the educational system; the party in its persuasive role-all that we have, in fact, called "the neo-Church."

The apparatus of economic exploitation: The monetary system; the banks; financial control; the stock exchange; management in industry.

Many political reformers wish to abolish some part of the unfree system. Republicans find the monarchy unnecessary. Secularists want to abolish the Church. Pacifists oppose the armed forces. Communists object to the apparatus of economic exploitation, at least, when it is not based upon the State. Cromwell dispensed with the legislature. Hitler made the judicature a farce.

Anarchists are unique in wishing to abolish all these forces of repression, and the police force in particular. For the police (or the army in a police role) is the cornerstone of the State. Without it the debates at Westminster become as sterile as those of the Oxford Union, and less interesting.

One organ of the State can seldom do the work of another. The Church has acted as a civil service and even as a police force (Jesuit state of Paraguay). The monarchy has been judge and jury. The banks often control the means of production. But, on the other hand, the monarchy could hardly save us from foreign invasion if it did not have an army (though some of its admirers have believed otherwise). The stock exchange would find it hard to persuade us that we are a free and independent people, and the police force, without a Church, would find it very difficult to get us into Heaven.

It is true that government takes over the control of certain necessary social functions. It does not follow that only the State could assume such control. The postmen are "civil servants" only because the State makes them such. The railways were not always run by the State. They belonged to the capitalists, and could as easily have been run by the railroad workers. The police find our lost dogs but that is because the registers are kept at police stations, not post offices.

There was an old superstition that if the Church excommunicated a country, it underwent a terrible disaster. There were grounds for this belief. At that time, only by the blessing of the Church could one be married, buried, leave property, do business in safety, be educated, or tended whilst sick. So long as people believed in the Church, the curse worked. A country banned from the communion of believers found its Church-run hospitals closed, and nobody dared take them over for fear of hell-fire. There was no trust in business, since the clerics administered oaths, and without the magic ritual there could be no credit granted. Education ceased, for the clergy ran the schools. Children could still, surprisingly to some, be begotten, but as they could not be christened, they were barred from the community of believers. They spent their lives in dread. Unmarried parents could not leave their property to their illegitimate children, and unless the Church reopened could not be married.

We are wiser now. But we have replaced one superstition by another. The opponents of anarchism assure us that if we put government under a ban, there would be no education, for the State controls the schools. There would be no hospitals—where would the money come from? Nobody would work—who would pay their wages? "There would not be a virgin or a rupee between Calcutta and Peshawar," the Anglo-Indians used smugly to assure those who would abolish the British Raj. For only the State prevented rape or robbery (a jest that savored of bitter wit in Nazi-occupied Europe).

But in reality, not the Church nor the State, but the people provide what the people have. If the people do not provide for themselves, the State cannot help them. It only appears to do so because it is in control. Those who have power may apportion work or regulate the standard of living, but this is part of the attack upon the people, not something undertaken on their behalf.

To consider whether the organs of repression are indispensable or not is the same as considering whether the enemy's armaments are dispensable or not. They are essential to *him* if he is to conquer. *We* can find arguments against them. *He* will seek to justify them. *We* should be convinced of the necessity for their abolition. In these terms, a free society is one in which the enemy is deprived of his weapons, or in other words, one in which repressive institutions are abolished or circumvented so as to be made useless.

We have seen in our time that it does not matter if a church lingers on as a historic curiosity, or even as a living body. It will seek to transform itself into a non-repressive body once it no longer has power. Other formerly repressive institutions that have lost their power try to adjust to the realities of the situation. Capitalism is nowhere more triumphant than in the City of London, but quaint medieval relics persist with no power but snobbery. A society would not be less free because some of its citizens voluntarily got together and contributed to a State, which exacted obedience from them. But such a demonstration of loyalty to the past would become as obsolescent as celebrating the fertility rite around the maypole. The latter is more natural than queuing up to pay taxes and might the better be regarded.

In the atmosphere of freedom, when coercive institutions have been made powerless and unnecessary, and public opinion can no longer be manufactured, parties advocating a return to the need for power will come to suffer the fate of all socially irrelevant or romantically outmoded lost causes. Having passed through an inquisition, people do not willingly go back to it. The horrors of the past become incapable of credulity, and must be forcibly imposed if the State finds them necessary again. For people rush to defend their freedom when it is openly attacked. Only under accepted, historic conquest do they become apathetic, for they do not understand its nature and are persuaded to accept it as inevitable.

No doubt in the early stages of a revolution it would be necessary, within clubs similar to those of the French Revolution, to prepare to strike down those who would reintroduce repression. Political parties would not disappear overnight. What would disappear would be the domination of political life by parties. The removal of the sweets of office would help to eliminate the desire for office. The notion of king-sacrifice may not have been an idle superstition of primitive society. Certainly in the first years of a free society, those consciously libertarian would need to assert the defense of freedom by sacrificing those who would rule. But in the space of a lifetime, freedom would be as necessary as the air we breathe.

The notion of a free society is so attractive as to be generally acceptable to all who are not completely warped by authority, and especially by successive younger generations, whenever imposed ideals of duty and obedience have cracked because too great sacrifices were demanded in their name. Against these notions can be seen the alternative possibilities arising from indiscipline and disobedience such as: the abolition of frontiers, fraternity between peoples, "one world, no government," the absence of war and end of violence, the breaking down of artificial class barriers, sexual liberation, education without forced discipline, and production for use not profit.

Indeed, all this, whether labeled anarchism or not, may be accepted as a useful package ideal, that is to say, as a fiction. Expressed as art, drama or literature, it can startle the bourgeoisie or even lull them. Inevitably, anarchism is expressed in relation to art, drama, literature, and music, just as religion, patriotism, and the party creeds have been. But the fictional representation should not be mistaken for the real thing.

It is an easy approach to libertarian thinking to express the iniquitous violence of the State, and contrast it with the complete non-violence of a non-governmental society. Yet it is dishonest to show the goods without mentioning the price, and a free society can only come about through determined resistance. It is not only a question of overthrowing a ruling class, but making it abundantly clear that no rule may exist again. The aim of the free society is not the "rejection" of the repressive organs of the State. It is their abolition.

In the realm of fiction, a revolutionary role is played by the creative writer, artist, musician. In the appreciation of their rejection of State values, the student plays a revolutionary role. But as regards the real thing, we have to consider in terms of the clash within society between those who rule and those who are ruled. It is a clash that amounts to civil war whether one calls it so or not. It is necessary to abolish imposed conquest in the realm both of the mind and of the body.

The psychological results of defeat are shown by fawning upon the conqueror, seeking to assimilate with him, and regarding his values as the only true ones. Only rarely does it become active resistance. More often it is apathy. This is seen graphically illustrated in national conquest, but exists in exactly the same way in social conquest. It is this type of apathy in defeat that is combated by individual action leading to the restoration of self-confidence (as seen in the Paris *attentats* in the decade after the defeat of the Commune). To say that a free society is chimerical is to say that repressive institutions are essential, and therefore that defeat is inevitable. The argument is dear to the hearts of those who desire power but wish to be loved while exercising it. They are only laboring "for our good" and not out of personal ambition. They would like us to have a non-competitive society, "but it won't work," and the only one that *will* work is one that lines their pockets. It would be pleasant to dispense with government, but "You have to keep *some* form of government (after all, liberty is not license)," and they are reluctantly prepared to sacrifice themselves in providing it.

For us, no repressive institutions have value except to the conquering minority. We do not think that when they are all gone, we will get utopia. We are not going to see utopia in our generation. Utopia we conceive as the standard by which we measure our actions, and the goal we may reach. The free society for us is a stage on the way and is immediately capable of achievement. Some might say, using the ideal as a block to action, that first there must be a revolution in men's minds before there could be a change in society. But to the revolutionary anarchist, the reverse is true. There must be a revolution in men's minds, and if this can precede social change so much the better. Without the economic base of society being radically altered the revolution in men's minds that will take us to utopia will be impossible. For such a revolution would face not only the brute force of the State but also the means of persuasion as a method of oppression. It is a good excuse to the police to say that the only revolution we were contemplating at the moment was to achieve the free society within our minds. Jesus is said to have made some such similar excuse to the Roman soldiers, but revolutionaries have got a lot bolder since then.

The expropriation of industry is not a remote possibility. Even today, control is in the hands of the workers. It is this control which the technological revolution would wrest away and by dispossessing the productive classes, create a new tyranny. There is always a degree of encroachment of control by labor upon industry. There is, too, a firm point beyond which such encroachment cannot possibly go, without the industry closing or being taken over by the workers. The occupation of factories in time of social unrest is another firm point beyond which the workers cannot go, without taking over industry. Once they begin to work again, but with management locked out, it ceases to be a strike, and becomes a revolution.

Seeing the revolution as a break with State-dominated society, we cease to be admirers of "progress," usually interpreted as the way things happen to have gone or the unchecked direction in which they are going. We look both backwards and forwards.

Backward, indeed, to the free city, with its guilds of craftsmen and groups of scholars, its folk-meeting and loose federal association. But forward to the use of technology in its proper place, at the service of man, with education helping to eradicate hatreds and not ingrain them. Backward to the natural countryside, the village not tarted up for stockbrokers to live in and the streams not polluted because of the need for profits. But forward to the liberation of the mind from the superstitions of the past, to the ending of sexual puritanism with the incursion of authority into the concerns of humanity. Backward to the society without rulers imposed by conquest. Forward to the society freed from the domination of government or the principle of exploitation. Backward to the workers' councils of the Russian and German revolutions; the free communes of Spain, Ukrainia, Mexico; the occupation of the places of work in France and Italy; the earliest aims of the British shop stewards' movement and the federalistic conceptions of the First International. Forward to the utopia of William Morris, now well within the reach of man.

Commentary on Names

(i) *Karl Marx* drew attention to the economic development of society and the nature of the class struggle; his socialism, although revolutionary, was based upon the State. Most of his followers, during his lifetime, believed the "capture of the State" to be based upon legalism, but after the Paris Commune, he made it clear that he believed in armed revolution. He never explained how the takeover would be effected nor what his conception of socialism was except that he believed in the "inevitability" of socialism (because capitalism was concentrating on larger units and the ever-increasing misery would cause the workers to rebel, take over the State, and nationalize the monopolies), a now-exploded theory.

(ii) *Mikhail Bakunin* progressed during his lifetime from the concept of democratic revolution, to adopting Proudhon's (xiii) federalism to the idea of socialism. Within the International (vi) he correctly envisaged that Marxian socialism would be "red Bismarckianism" and that state socialism would be a new tyranny. after the Paris Commune, his theories developed into revolutionary anarchism.

(iii) *Herbert Read*, English art critic and philosopher, adapted anarchist ideas to surrealism, literature, and education. Although he remained essentially a liberal in his attitude to present-day society, his conceptions of a free society are a valuable guide to utopia.

(iv) *Henrik Ibsen*, the Norwegian playwright, was regarded by anarchists such as Emma Goldman to be the dramatic prophet of the libertarian movement, though it is fair to say that Bernard Shaw, taking identical texts, has portrayed him as the dramatic prophet of authoritarian socialism.

(v) *Peter Kropotkin*, Russian writer and former prince, after living among Swiss workers, adapted the general principles of revolutionary anarchism to the labor movement, and set out to show that it rested upon a scientific basis.

(vi) *The First International* was a reflection of the views then current in the labor movement, including: Marxist socialism-and its parliamentary offshoot, German social democracy; French and Swiss Proudhonism, which Bakunin helped to develop into anarchism; English trade-unionism; the Republicanism of Garibaldi (conquest of democratic power by armed force) and the ideas of Blanqui (conquest of socialism by the same method, which influenced Lenin's later theories and is today seen reflected in the Che Guevara cult).

(vii) *Percy Bysshe Shelley*, the poet, is often thought of as a libertarian revolutionary, which does not bear too much analysis. He was the son-in-law of William Godwin, whose views on the stateless society make him in one line the predecessor of anarchism, and in another line the predecessor of laissez-faire liberalism.

(viii) *Daniel Cohn-Bendit* has become the accepted spokesman for the French student rebellion against authoritarian society.

(ix) *Herbert Marcuse* has been elected by the press to be the theorist of fashionable radicalism.

(x) *Leon Trotsky* was a social-democrat who became minister of war in the Bolshevik government, and as such was responsible for the repression of the Kronstadt sailors and the Ukrainian peasants who tried to make "free soviets" into a reality. Afterwards, he himself was forced into opposition by Joseph Stalin, and he became a fierce critic of "the bureaucracy" without admitting it to be a separate class.

(xi) *Vladimir Lenin*, although a Marxist, staggered social-democratic theory by his denunciation of the State; although in practice he still followed the Marxian principle of conquest of the State, he claimed it would "wither away." When the State ceased to be the "executive committee of the bourgeoisie," those organs of the State that guarded economic repression "withered away," but since it became the "executive committee" of the bureaucracy, the other repressive institutions became stronger than ever.

(xii) *The Bolsheviki* (majority) as opposed to the Mensheviki (minority) were part of the Russian social-democratic movement until the split over support for the First World War. In matters of theory there were no differences between German and Russian social-democrats who were split much upon the same lines. Both were Marxist socialists of the authoritarian brand. British social democracy, however, was diluted by trade unionism and Methodism, and finally fashioned by Fabianism.

(xiii) *Pierre-Joseph Proudhon* was a French federalist philosopher, who coined the name "anarchist" in its present sense, presuming that if government were necessary, "anarchy" could be used to mean chaos and confusion, but that if government were not necessary, "anarchy" (the absence of government) meant complete liberty. Only the authoritarian, he held, could believe that complete liberty meant chaos. In this sense he is the "father" of anarchism though not, in the modern sense, an anarchist himself. He pioneered the exposition of French working-class autonomous organization.

(xiv) *A.S. Neill* is the modem pioneer of libertarian education and of "hearts not heads in the school." Though he has denied being an anarchist, it would be hard to know how else to describe his philosophy, though he is correct in recognizing the difference between revolution in philosophy and pedagogy, and the revolutionary change of society. They are associated but not the same thing.

(xv) *The CNT-FAI* (National Confederation of Labor, anarcho-syndicalist; Iberian Anarchist Federation) was the driving force in the Spanish Revolution of 1936 which was associated with the social revolutionary changes in the economy, behind the Republican lines, until this was smashed by the Communist Party, aided by Russian arms, a year or so before the Stalin-Hitler Pact.

(xvi) *The Chicago Martyrs* (referred to in the song of the "Red Flag") were anarchists, framed by the Chicago police on capital charges in

1886 and heralded as martyrs of the class war. They are associated with the first celebrations of May Day as a workers' day.

(xvii) *Sacco and Vanzetti* were Italian-American anarchists, framed in the 1920s, again on a capital charge, who also became symbols of the class struggle.

(xviii) *Joe Hill*, of the Industrial Workers of the World, was yet another martyr of the class struggle, hanged by the State of Utah. His songs have become folklore.

(xix) *Rudi Dutschke* was the spokesman of the German student left until shot at by a reactionary.

(xx) The *Spartacists* were the council communists of Germany who, rejecting the Party dogmatism of social-democracy, realized that the workers' councils that were springing up all over the country were the means by which the new society "would grow within the framework of the old."

(xxi) The *Fabians* took Marxism to its logical conclusion, and visualized a society dominated by do-gooders from the middle classes. They permeated first the Liberal Party, then the Labor Party, and transformed the labor movement into one dominated by the "professional class." With the comparative political success of British "socialism," French socialism followed the same disastrous course, which left the Communist Party the only party in France even pretending to be working-class.

(xxii) *Fernand Pelloutier* was the pioneer of French syndicalist theory, and the conception that the workers' organizations could control industry. He is in direct contrast to the British trade union leaders who felt it was necessary to have political connections.

(xxiii) The *Industrial Workers of the World (IWW)* was American syndicalism. It threw off the early De Leonist conception of "political power," seeing this as a method by which the middle class would retain dominance. It saw no purpose in political action, and insisted on direct action for industrial power. It grew in extent and militancy until the reactionary period following the First World War and if "dead," it has obstinately refused "to lie down."

(xxiv) *Daniel De Leon* gave Marxism an understanding of how socialism could be achieved, relating it more directly to the class struggle. His conception was of political power as well as economic power; the Party to seize the State, the workers to seize industry. Lenin owed a great deal to De Leon.

(xxv) *Ferdinand Lassalle* made a melange of Marxism, legalism, and demagogy into the first German workers' movement. He might be said to be equally the father of present-day social democracy and of Nazism, with his mixture of patriotism and socialism, mass labor movements and small concentrated leadership. His theory of the Iron Law of Wages became the subject of general derision after its demolition by socialists. It held that all increases in wages and benefits under capitalism must mean increases in prices, and therefore ultimately increases in poverty. This fallacy has now become fashionable once again under the Labor government.

(xxvi) *Rosa Luxemburg* tried to reconcile revolutionary social democracy with council communism. Her death at the hands of German reactionaries came too soon for the inconsistencies in her thought to be made plain.

(xxvii) The *Social Revolutionary* Movement of Russia was not (as is sometimes supposed) either nihilist or anarchist, nor were the latter two synonymous. The social-revolutionaries looked on the peasantry as the class of the revolution in the same way that the social democrats looked on the industrial worker. The social-revolutionaries were dedicated opponents of the czarists, and in particular their womenfolk (like the English suffragettes, in many ways) were courageous and active. The nihilists were simply democrats who wished to end czarism. Unlike social-revolutionaries and anarchists they did not use "terrorism."

(xxviii) *Errico Malatesta* was one of the best-known popularizers of anarchist theory (cf. V. Richards, *Malatesta: His Life and Thought*, Freedom Press).

(xxix) *Nestor Makhno* organized a peasant army in the Ukraine which established free communes. At one time Lenin was prepared to "let the anarchists try out their theories" in the Ukraine but the territory was too valuable (and the example too contagious) for this to be done. The Makhnovists fought both Red troops and Whites. Trotsky made peace with them so that the Red Army could join with them in driving out the czarists, but afterwards turned on them to establish state communism. Makhno has subsequently been the most maligned of all Russian revolutionaries, a process set in motion by Trotsky who later found it used against himself by Stalin.

(xxx) *William Morris* is the visionary of utopia in the English labor tradition.

(xxxi) *CND* (the Campaign for Nuclear Disarmament) and its offshoot the nonviolent direct-actionist Committee of Hundred, began as a protest against the Destruction State that unexpectedly drew wide support and became the focal point of protest for a new generation. The belief of some of its founders that "they did it all", and the pretentious claims associated with it, may be ignored.

(xxxii) *James Connolly* was a socialist of the De Leon school and an Irish patriot.

(xxxiii) *Henry David Thoreau*, American individualist, has often been regarded as an anarchist of an idyllic school ("a gentle anarchist," in journalistic cant). His attitudes are probably the most typical of what would be advanced liberalism and non-involvement in the present society.

Endnotes

1   See Commentary on Names at the end of the book.
2   Herbert Read, *To Hell with Culture* (London and New York: Routledge, 2002) 180.
3   Letter on his seventieth birthday to a meeting in Carnegie Hall, New York, 1912. Emma Goldman, *Living My Life*, vol. 2 (New York: Dover, 1970) 510.
4   Petr Kropotkin, *Fields, Factories and Workshops* (New York: Putnam, 1913) 408.
5   Charles Kingsley, *His Letters and Memoirs of His Life, Edited by His Wife* (London: MacMillan, 1921) 63-64.
6   The "Clyde Revolt" was a foretaste of a British revolution.
7   See Icarus [pseud.], *The Wilhelmshaven Revolt: A Chapter of the Revolutionary Movement in the German Navy, 1918-1919* (London: Freedom Press, 1944); Raden [pseud.] *The Origins of the Movement for Workers' Councils in Germany, 1918-35,* (London: Coptic Press, 1968).
8   Andy Anderson, *Hungary 56* (London: Solidarity, 1964).
9   For some account of the background, see Internationalist, *The Origins of the Anarchist Movement in China* by (London: Coptic Press, 1968).
10   See Gerald Brenan, *The Spanish Labyrinth: An Account of the Social and Political Background of the Civil War* (Cambridge: Cambridge University Press, 1950).
11   For a description of the process, see *The Russian Anarchists* by Paul Avrich (Oakland: AK Press, 2005).
12   It is possible to be a nationalist and a socialist. James Connolly (xxxii) was. As a nation implies a State, it is not possible to be

a nationalist and an anarchist. The hybrid word *national-social-ist* means something as different from Connolly as chalk from cheese, though to be sure it has elements of both nationalism and state socialism. So too the hybrid *pacifist-anarchist* means something different from pacifism and anarchism.

13 The French Revolution, and the English Civil War, were seen as risings by the inferior races against their natural masters. The Jews were not (until the Nuremberg Laws) classed as an "inferior race" but as one that had obtained world domination and was especially dangerous to the German "helots" without their "Aryan" masters. "Aryanism" was a conception similar to that of "Norman blood," a ruling section within the nation.

14 This is why separatist nationalism and decentralism are often confused.

15 The Social-Revolutionary Stepniak, recounting this incident in King Log and King Stork, and evidently believing in the "power" of Rothschild and other Jewish financiers, was unable to understand why they allowed the Czar to continue the pogroms. But presenting dishonored bonds, in which all religions believed, was one thing. Presenting the case of dishonored humanity was quite another. On such an issue, everyone spoke different languages.

16 Those on both sides of the House who like to believe this are apt to quote Burke to prove that they do not have to consider what their constituents think of the measures they pass, as if this reactionary politician's opinions had bound the British people for evermore.

17 The Spanish anarchist movement did in fact send representatives into the Republican government during the Civil War, fearing that the exclusion of working-class movements would lead to Communist Party domination. But their ministers in the Cabinet ceased to be revolutionary, and called for compromise with the government (including the communists).

18 The Roman Church was once said to be what the Communist Party has since become, "a lamb in adversity, a fox in equality, a tiger in supremacy."

19 cf. the Socialist Party of Great Britain (Fitzgeraldites) for an interesting illustration. It broke from the old Social Democrat Federation sixty years ago, adopted a programme based on the bowdlerized version of Marx then current, and has remained static ever since.

20 We are well aware that a libertarian can do whatever he chooses. It is not, however, by moral standards that one judges a revolutionary, but by actions. If we say that a total abstainer cannot drink whisky any more than beer, we are not laying down a rule but making a definition.

21 The Independent Labor Party, for instance, has a fortune of over a million sterling. It is a memorial to past struggles. The party has become a minor and forgotten sect. Its trustees sit on the cashbox like immovable buddhas. Yet if the money were allowed to be controlled by the party, the party would be flooded by outside elements coming in. It is often subject to attempted takeovers (CP, Trotskyists, Maoists etc.), which only the faceless bureaucracy has defeated.

22 See E. P. Thompson, *The Making of the English Working Class* (New York: Pantheon, 1964). "Luddism," incidentally, comes not from a Ned Ludd, if he ever existed, but from King Lud, the mythical British king commemorated in Ludgate Circus in London. The evocation of his name brought back the idea of a happy past before "the conquest," the idealized medieval past and a craftsman's utopia freed from those who had come to rule.

> As the liberty lads o'er the sea,
> Bought their freedom, and cheaply, with blood,
> So we, boys, we, will die fighting, or live free,
> And down with all kings but King Ludd!
> (Lord Byron, "Song for the Luddites," 1816)

23 See Mikhail Bakunin, *God and the State* (New York: Dover, 1970).

24 For a fascinating glimpse of how juvenile the scientific mind can sometimes be, outside its proper sphere, see the exchange of letters between Freud and Einstein on the causes of war; an ephemeral publication of the thirties. Einstein emotionally appeals to Freud to use his science to prove war to be wrong, and Freud explains that it is part of the human psyche. Neither has the least idea of its cause.

25 Correspondence in *The Times*, following the publication of *Killing No Murder* by Edward Hyams, revealed the true attitude of the establishment. Apparently Hitler could have been assassinated and plans were submitted. But individual killing of leaders (as distinct from dissidents) was "always murder" and could have "undesirable repercussions." Presumably the Second World War was a "desirable" repercussion.

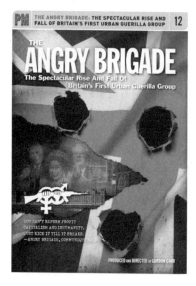

The Angry Brigade:
The Spectacular Rise and Fall of
Britain's First Urban
Guerilla Group
DVD
978-1-60486-196-9
$19.95

Between 1970 and 1972 the Angry Brigade used guns and bombs in a series of symbolic attacks against property. A series of communiqués accompanied the actions, explaining the choice of targets and the Angry Brigade philosophy: autonomous organization and attacks on property alongside other forms of militant working class action. Targets included the embassies of repressive regimes, police stations and army barracks, boutiques and factories, government departments and the homes of Cabinet ministers, the Attorney General and the Commissioner of the Metropolitan Police. These attacks on the homes of senior political figures increased the pressure for results and brought an avalanche of police raids. From the start the police were faced with the difficulty of getting to grips with a section of society they found totally alien. And were they facing an organization—or an idea?

This documentary, produced by Gordon Carr for the BBC (and first shown in January 1973, shortly after the trial), covers the roots of the Angry Brigade in the revolutionary ferment of the 1960s, and follows their campaign and the police investigation to its culmination in the "Stoke Newington 8" conspiracy trial at the Old Bailey—the longest criminal trial in British legal history. Produced after extensive research—among both the libertarian opposition and the police—it remains the essential study of Britain's first urban guerilla group.

Extra: *The Persons Unknown* (1980, 22 minutes)
The so-called "Persons Unknown" case in which members of the Anarchist Black Cross were tried (and later acquitted) at the Old Bailey on charges of "conspiring with persons unknown, at places unknown, to cause explosions and to overthrow society." Featuring interviews and footage of Stuart Christie, Nicholas Walter, Crass and many other UK anarchist activists and propagandists of the time.

Gordon Carr

The Angry Brigade: A History of Britain's First Urban Guerilla Group
Gordon Carr
978-1-60486-049-8
$24.95

"You can't reform profit capitalism and inhumanity. Just kick it till it breaks."
— Angry Brigade, communiqué.

Between 1970 and 1972, the Angry Brigade used guns and bombs in a series of symbolic attacks against property. A series of communiqués accompanied the actions, explaining the choice of targets and the Angry Brigade philosophy: autonomous organization and attacks on property alongside other forms of militant working class action. Targets included the embassies of repressive regimes, police stations and army barracks, boutiques and factories, government departments and the homes of Cabinet ministers, the Attorney General and the Commissioner of the Metropolitan Police. These attacks on the homes of senior political figures increased the pressure for results and brought an avalanche of police raids. From the start the police were faced with the difficulty of getting to grips with a section of society they found totally alien. And were they facing an organization—or an idea?

This book covers the roots of the Angry Brigade in the revolutionary ferment of the 1960s, and follows their campaign and the police investigation to its culmination in the "Stoke Newington 8" conspiracy trial at the Old Bailey—the longest criminal trial in British legal history. Written after extensive research—among both the libertarian opposition and the police—it remains the essential study of Britain's first urban guerilla group.

This expanded edition contains a comprehensive chronology of the "Angry Decade," extra illustrations and a police view of the Angry Brigade. Introductions by Stuart Christie and John Barker (two of the "Stoke Newington 8" defendants) discuss the Angry Brigade in the political and social context of its times—and its longer-term significance.

Arena Two: Noir Fiction
Stuart Christie, series editor
978-1-60486-214-0
$14

Arena Two taps into the rich seam of anarchists in fiction, and anarchist/libertarian noir authors. This second volume focuses on books with atmospheric qualities that are dark and sinister—but not without hope. Their protagonists, some with profoundly flawed personalities, have something of the romantic optimist about them; men and women driven to face moral challenges and to do battle with the forces of evil or plain banality. They live in a world where natural justice isn't part of the landscape.

Authors looked at include: Diego R. Barbosa (of the *Novela Ideal* series), Stig Dagerman, Andre Helena, Leo Malet, George Navel, Jean-Marc Raynaud, Leda Rafanelli, B. Traven, and Simone Weil. There are also reviews by Agustin Guillamon of Miguel Mir's *Entre El Roig I El Negre* (supposed memoirs found in London of a FAI gunman) and by Massimo Ortalli on a 1923 novel published by a Salesian friar, *The Regeneration of An Anarchist* (imprisoned anarchist finds God and recommits his life) with extracts from the original. The issue also examines the relationship between surrealism and anarchism with articles by Simon Watson Taylor and Stephen Schwartz.

Arena One: On Anarchist Cinema
Richard Porton, guest editor
978-1-60486-050-4
$14

In the wake of the end of the Cold War and worldwide protests against corporate globalization, anarchism continues to attract new adherents among both aging leftists and new generations of young radicals. *Arena* aims to tap into this revived interest in libertarian ideas, culture and practice by providing a dynamic focal point: a journal that brings together good, stimulating and provocative writing and scholarship on libertarian culture of all kinds.

Designed for a general, intelligent, popular readership as well as for scholars and aficionados working in the area, the first issue of *Arena* focuses on film and video—historical and modern—and future issues will cover the entire spectrum of the arts: film, theatre, and art criticism as well as political theory and practice, reportage, letters, reviews, and unpublished fiction and nonfiction.

FRIENDS OF

PM

IN THE TWO YEARS SINCE its founding—and on a mere shoestring—PM Press has risen to the formidable challenge of publishing and distributing knowledge and entertainment for the struggles ahead. With over 40 releases in 2009, we have published an impressive and stimulating array of literature, art, music, politics, and culture. Using every available medium, we've succeeded in connecting those hungry for ideas and information to those putting them into practice.

Friends of PM allows you to directly help impact, amplify, and revitalize the discourse and actions of radical writers, filmmakers, and artists. It provides us with a stable foundation from which we can build upon our early successes and provides a much-needed subsidy for the materials that can't necessarily pay their own way. You can help make that happen—and receive every new title automatically delivered to your door once a month—by joining as a Friend of PM Press. Here are your options:

- • $25 a month: Get all books and pamphlets plus 50% discount on all webstore purchases.
- • $25 a month: Get all CDs and DVDs plus 50% discount on all webstore purchases.
- • $40 a month: Get all PM Press releases plus 50% discount on all webstore purchases
- • $100 a month: Superstar—Everything plus PM merchandise, free downloads, and 50% discount on all webstore purchases.

For those who can't afford $25 or more a month, we're introducing Sustainer Rates at $15, $10 and $5. Sustainers get a free PM Press t-shirt and a 50% discount on all purchases from our website.

Just go to **WWW.PMPRESS.ORG** to sign up. Your card will be billed once a month, until you tell us to stop. Or until our efforts succeed in bringing the revolution around. Or the financial meltdown of Capital makes plastic redundant. Whichever comes first.

PM PRESS was founded at the end of 2007 by a small collection of folks with decades of publishing, media, and organizing experience. PM co-founder Ramsey Kanaan started AK Press as a young teenager in Scotland almost 30 years ago and, together with his fellow PM Press coconspirators, has published and distributed hundreds of books, pamphlets, CDs, and DVDs. Members of PM have founded enduring book fairs, spearheaded victorious tenant organizing campaigns, and worked closely with bookstores, academic conferences, and even rock bands to deliver political and challenging ideas to all walks of life. We're old enough to know what we're doing and young enough to know what's at stake.

We seek to create radical and stimulating fiction and nonfiction books, pamphlets, t-shirts, visual and audio materials to entertain, educate and inspire you. We aim to distribute these through every available channel with every available technology - whether that means you are seeing anarchist classics at our bookfair stalls; reading our latest vegan cookbook at the café; downloading geeky fiction e-books; or digging new music and timely videos from our website.

PM PRESS is always on the lookout for talented and skilled volunteers, artists, activists and writers to work with. If you have a great idea for a project or can contribute in some way, please get in touch.

PM PRESS
PO Box 23912
Oakland CA 94623
510-658-3906
www.pmpress.org